Self-catering France

JOHN P. HARRIS AND WILLIAM HEDLEY

Illustrated by Penny Quested

D0552920

HarperCollins*Publishers*
New York
London and Glasgow

The Authors
Since moving to France with his wife almost twenty years
ago, John P. Harris has written for *Le Monde*, *The Times* and
other publications in France and the UK. He is now known for his
accounts of life as *An Englishman in the Midi* on BBC Radio 4, and is
currently preparing a guide to the Loire, to be published by Collins.
William Hedley used to teach in London but moved to France
with his young family in 1988. He has written on a wide
range of subjects for British book publishers and
newspapers. Each author has contributed
chapters to this book.

Edited and designed by the Book Creation Company Limited,
1 Newburgh Street, London W1V 1LH

Series concept: Jackie Jones
Editors: Sydney Francis, Eileen Cadman
Design: Christine Wood
Index: Hilary Bird
Research: Emma Hurd, David Johnston
Typesetting: Columns, Reading
Printed in Hong Kong

Published by HarperCollins*Publishers*

The Book Creation Company wishes to thank Pepita Aris
for her invaluable help with the recipes, and Ros Schwartz
for checking the French.

British Library Cataloguing in Publication Data
Harris, John P.
   France. – (Collins self-catering)
   1.France. Visitors' guides
   I. Title II. Hedley, William
   914.404839

   ISBN 0-00-436104-0

While every care has been taken in the preparation of this book,
neither the authors nor publishers can accept any liability
for any consequence arising from the use of information
contained herein.

CONTENTS

CHAPTER ONE

INTRODUCTION

Everything is easier and more fun if you can speak the language, but in the village where I live I've met *gîte*-renting foreigners who knew no French at all. They managed fine, going out each day in their car to swim and windsurf in the lake 8km (5 miles) away, or in the sea 32km (20 miles) away. They did all their shopping at the local supermarket, and often ate at a restaurant in the nearest town where the waiter spoke English.

Having said that, you'll have a much more interesting holiday if you are not deaf and dumb most of the time. There's no need to be uptight about this; memories of school grammatical exercises can be inhibiting. Forget about the problem of *writing* French (which the French find tricky, too) although it helps to be able to read as much as possible and to be able to transfer words from print to speech. Vocabulary is the thing, with a willingness to have a go. The French are as lazy as the British about learning foreign languages, but they are almost all subjected to English classes at school. A conversation in a mixture of French and English, helped by gestures, might score zero marks in a school exam, but this is real life and, if it works, it passes the test.

For a start, you can get by with *bonjour* (hello), *merci* (thank-you), *au revoir* (goodbye) and a warm smile. Take a phrase book with you, and use the phrases given in this book. If you don't understand, say '*Je ne comprends pas*' and, as a last resort, '*Parlez-vous anglais?*' ('Do you speak English?')

One couple we know came to our village ten years ago. They knew very little French, but they enjoyed themselves and took an interest in the local goings-on. When they got back to England they went to evening classes in spoken French. Then they came again. And again, and again. They're retired now, but they still come every year. They keep up with their French in England, with more advanced classes and membership of a French circle, and they are welcomed as friends every year in the village. Their first self-catering holiday in France was the start of an absorbing new interest. Perhaps that's the right attitude.

FRENCH HOLIDAY HABITS

The French are a prominent feature of France, and their presence and habits will make a difference, pro and con, to your holiday. So here are a few statistics to help you plan. This is when they go away in summer: 6% in May, 9% in June, 37% in July, 40% in August and 8% in September. Of these, nearly half go to the coast, and over a third choose the mountains and countryside. The remainder go to towns or tour around seeing new parts of their big, fascinating country. The moral: if you want to rent accommodation in July or August, especially if you are heading for the coast, you had better book very early, or resign yourself to taking something pricey.

If you are driving, bear in mind that three-quarters of the French go on holiday in their cars. So, although there are many more miles of good road per car in France than in Britain, you are likely to find heavy traffic and bottlenecks on motorways and main roads in France at the peak summer points: the weekends at the beginning, middle and end of both July and August.

So . . . outside July and August, France is your oyster for self-catering holidays, especially in the country. The facilities are there waiting for you, and the natives will be friendly. If the owner of your *gîte* doesn't roll out the red carpet for you, at least he'll open the red wine. But in high season, book early or see what a British agency can offer, especially if you want to be able to walk to a good beach. And drive there *very* carefully. Too many French holidaymakers start by driving much too far, too long and too fast. You wouldn't do that, would you?

HOW TO USE THIS BOOK

You'll find that *Self-catering in France* is useful at all stages of thinking about your holiday: making plans and organizing, travelling, and once you get there.

The first few chapters will help you during the preparatory stages. Chapter 2 describes self-catering in France in a general way; a brief guide to the different regions is followed by a description of the types of self-catering accommodation available, how much they're likely to cost, and what facilities are likely to be provided (or not). There's also a special section for those with children. Chapter 3 covers the various ways of finding a suitable self-catering property, including an extensive (but not exhaustive) list of companies that offer self-catering holidays in France, and the pros and cons of the various travel options. Chapter 4 lists everything you need to think about when preparing to travel abroad – passports, insurance, currency, health – with useful checklists of things that it's easy to forget.

The book then moves on to what you can expect when you arrive. It describes what happens when you take possession of a self-catering property, and includes useful phrases and vocabulary.

Chapter 6 approaches the heart of the self-catering holiday with a look at French habits and customs concerning food and drink. The various beverages (both alcoholic and non-alcoholic) are described, followed by a trip through the different types of French restaurants and bars and what they serve, for the evenings when you'd rather eat out.

Chapter 7 will give you an excellent start to the adventure of shopping (take this book with you when you go). It describes the shops and markets and the type of food you'll find in them – dairy products, vegetables, meat, fish, groceries, and more. Chapter 8 is the core of the book for self-caterers. Here there's a wide range of simple menus (with the shopping list in French alongside), including meals that need almost no preparation, only a visit to the local shop. Eating like the locals doesn't mean spending hours and hours slaving over a hot stove in the kitchen.

A big worry for some people can be taking children: Will they eat the food? Can you get nappies? How do restaurants react to them? Chapter 9 will reassure you on these points, and provides other practical information about taking children.

The following two chapters – on housekeeping, survival shopping, local services and health – are packed with advice and information on how to keep problems to a minimum, and what to do when things *do* go wrong. Since most self-caterers are likely to have a car, Chapter 11 contains a section on driving that gives basic information about the French rules of the road, and what to do if your car breaks down.

Although you're going on holiday to get away from it all, it may be necessary for you to keep in touch with friends or relatives at home. A section in Chapter 11 tells you how to make sure that you can be contacted, and how you can contact them if necessary.

While this book strives to be optimistic, it's as well to be prepared in case of emergencies, and Chapter 12 provides brief but necessary practical information about how to cope if one arises. On a happier note, you'll probably want to bring back something to remind you of your trip, and Chapter 13 gives a general description of the enormous variety of things you can buy.

CHAPTER TWO

THINKING OF GOING

SELF-CATERING IN FRANCE

Despite the fact that the standard of living in France is somewhat higher than in Britain as measured by the Gross National Product per head, and the fact that renting decent self-catering accommodation there is remarkably easy, *and* the fact that anyway you're not far from home if something goes disastrously wrong – despite all that, self-catering in France can be a real adventure if you set out to 'go native' as far as you can manage. With average luck, nice surprises will outnumber nasty ones. You need a bit of know-how, though – and that's what this book is for.

Self-catering holidays are a well-established feature of normal French life. The average French worker gets five weeks' paid holiday per year, usually taken in two or three goes. Over half of the population takes a summer holiday away from home, lasting on average 24 days. Nearly all (82%) spend their holidays in France, but only 5% go to hotels: the rest prefer to cater for themselves in one way or another. Of these, 25% go to stay with relations or friends. Another 25% go to their own holiday houses in the country or by the sea (the French are great buyers of *résidences secondaires* – self-catering holidays plus a hoped-for inflation-proof investment) or borrow someone else's. A further 20% go camping or caravanning, and 20% rent short-let accommodation – flats by the sea, holiday villas and cottages. Some of these are grouped in *villages de vacances*. Far more are of the *gîte rural* type (see ACCOMMODATION in this chapter). So, if you decide to take the plunge, you will not be breaking the ice, but following a trail blazed by millions of French people.

REGIONAL GUIDE

Every holiday plan depends on the answers to certain questions. You've decided to go to France, but maybe not yet on the region. So, are you looking for the sun? Do you want to be near the sea? Are you interested in sightseeing? Architecture? Galleries? Concerts? Country walks?

France is a huge and varied country, and a proper survey would take up a whole book in itself, but the following outline should help you to narrow down the choices and decide which regions you'd like to investigate further.

Paris has been left out altogether. It is one of the world's finest cities but, like many cities, lack of accommodation makes it impractical for the self-caterer. If you find yourself within striking distance, however, it would be a crime not to visit Paris for a day or two.

THE NORTH

In practice, most British tourists are going to do no more than pass through the northernmost region of France on their way elsewhere. This is pity, perhaps, especially if history, museums and architecture interest you. Amiens has a superb Gothic cathedral, and there are other fine churches in nearby towns. There are also the beach resorts such as Le Touquet.

Visitors to Brittany certainly get away from it all. Dominated by the sea, the region has few large centres west of Rennes, and driving to and within Brittany can be slow and tortuous. Your own favourite items may be less easy to find there than in more populous regions, but the Bretons have to live, just like us, so you will find everything that you need. Even the smallest villages are within reach of basic food supplies, or are served by travelling shops.

Brittany's main centres are found on the coast – Brest and Quimper, for example – and the towns on the dramatic Emerald Coast, such as St Malo. Mont-Saint-Michel is a well-known tourist attraction, and the many beaches, more bracing than sun-kissed, perhaps, are very attractive indeed.

Less remote than Brittany, Normandy provides a perfect balance between peaceful, idyllic countryside, lively towns and fascinating history, including, of course, the Normandy landing beaches of the Second World War. The climate is mild. The main centres are Rouen (a city of 500,000 people), Cherbourg, Caen and Le Havre. It's a noted gastronomic centre, famous for the richness of its dairy produce, and varied food of the highest quality is easily found. The towns already mentioned have a wide range of out-of-town shopping facilities, and the smaller centres are usually excellent for day-to-day requirements.

Unlike the famous drink that comes from the region, much of Champagne is flat and chalky, but the countryside around Reims, the Côte des Blancs and the Vallée de la Marne is enchanting. Large areas of Reims itself were destroyed in the Second World War, but the superb cathedral survived, and the rebuilt city is bright and full of life. Other centres well worth a visit are Epernay, Troyes and Colombey-les-Deux-Eglises, where you can visit De Gaulle's house. And, of course, there's the champagne.

Alsace lies on the border between France and Germany and is separated from Lorraine, to the west, by the Vosges mountains, on which you can ski. The main centres are Strasbourg, Nancy and Metz, all of which are attractive cities in their own right and offer full shopping and other facilities. Other attractions of this region are the spas, such as Vittel, where you can take the waters – or, if you prefer, drink them.

CENTRAL FRANCE

The valley of France's longest river, the Loire, provides the setting for one of the most popular regions for tourists. The famous *châteaux*, not all of which are on the Loire itself, are a major attraction, but there are many small towns and villages that are enchanting in their own right. Nantes and, working east, Angers, Tours and Orléans, are the key centres in what is a very large geographical area. The Loire valley is an outstanding place to visit, but inevitably suffers from the influx of tourists in the high season.

A trip to Burgundy is likely to attract the lover of peace and quiet, the countryside and fine wines. It is a large region of mainly agricultural land. The only centre of any real size is Dijon, an impressive university town that is well worth a visit and offers first-rate shopping and other facilities.

In winter, the French Alps form part of one of the great skiing centres. There are many resorts throughout the region – La Plagne, Les Arcs and Megève, for example – but you'll need to check that there's good all-round skiing for you and your family. If you're not into skiing, the mountains in the summer are spectacular. The scenery is fabulous, the towns lovely and full of geraniums, and there's also a wide variety of activities, such as tennis, swimming and even paragliding for the more adventurous among you. Chamonix is a pretty and fascinating town, and Mont Blanc, which towers above it, is one of the world's greatest natural sights. Self-catering accommodation is widely available, but the region as a whole is rather fashionable, and therefore tends to be expensive.

THE SOUTH

Cognac and Bordeaux sound like items on a wine list, and the whole region is a delight for those who like to investigate the fruit of the vine and its bi-products. Bordeaux itself is a large, sophisticated city which, in spite of its attractive and picturesque corners, is essentially a business centre. It is excellent for shopping, eating, drinking and nightlife in general, and a good antidote for those who miss the town if they are away from it for too long. Further north is Cognac. (Brandy may only be called cognac if the grapes from which it was produced grew in a particular area just outside the town.)

Needless to say, a visit is almost bound to involve the tasting, if not the buying, of some of the local produce.

The Atlantic coast was once one of the most fashionable places in the world to enjoy the sun, the sea and the sand. It's a little faded now in places, but Biarritz still has its glamour, and St Jean de Luz is a pretty little resort a stone's throw from the Spanish border, in the heart of Basque country. Biarritz is expensive, but the further north you go, the more reasonable are the prices. What you lose in glitz you gain in space and tranquillity, although there are several resorts along the whole of this coast with attractive beaches and water sports. Inland there is the Parc Naturel des Landes de Gascoigne, and also Roquefort, where the famous cheese is made.

The Dordogne deserves a special mention, and not only because it has been a favourite with the British for many years. Périgueux and Bergerac are both well worth a visit, and Riberac is a pretty little town where you might see more British number-plates than French ones. British people also live in the region in large numbers, attracted, perhaps, by the scenery, which is very green, rolling, and rather English.

The Cathars were a medieval Christian sect whose unorthodox views led to many troubles and wars. In the region around Carcassonne, there are many fortified *châteaux* of Cathar origin; some are difficult to reach on foot, but very rewarding indeed when you do. Carcassonne itself is a good, modern shopping city with, on its outskirts, the remarkable medieval walled city in a state of almost perfect preservation. Along the motorway to the west is the pretty town of Castelnaudary, its lovely buildings rising up from a basin in the Canal du Midi, which flows through the town. Further west still brings you to the bustling and cosmopolitan city of Toulouse.

East of Carcassonne lies the Mediterranean, with its specially built coastal resorts and its fascinating coastal and inland cities, Perpignan, Narbonne, Montpellier, Nîmes and Arles, where Roman remains provide one of many reasons for a visit. This is a richly fascinating area of France, and one that is only just beginning to be exploited for tourists. As a result it tends to be relatively inexpensive (away from the coast, at any rate).

Continuing along the coast brings you to the playground of France, the Côte d'Azur. The famous resorts of St Tropez, Nice and Cannes have a glamour that few people can resist. They tend to be very crowded in the summer, and very expensive, and many people prefer them out of season when they demonstrate quite a different kind of charm. Turn inland to the heart of Provence and you'll find some of the most beautiful scenery in the whole of France. The countryside is quite stunning, and towns like Aix-en-Provence, Avignon and Orange are unrivalled in beauty and atmosphere.

Corsica is a rugged, scented antidote to the elegance and wealth of the South of France. It is a mountainous island, and indeed, the mountains are perhaps the best place to be in the height of summer, when the temperatures can go through the roof. Spring and autumn are good times to visit Corsica, as is the winter, when the temperatures at sea-level are often mild and pleasant, though the mountain passes may be blocked with snow. Ajaccio, the capital and one of the main ports, is bustling, lively and unsophisticated.

ACCOMMODATION

As far as accommodation is concerned, what you get depends on the nature of the region. For example, rural France is full of stone houses, and it is these that make up the bulk of self-catering accommodation in the countryside. The cost varies, of course, and here the region does make a difference. It's neither the beauty, the convenience nor the facilities which bump up the cost, but the level to which the region has been developed for tourists. So a house in the Provençal country-side will be considerably more expensive than the same kind of thing around Castelnaudary, yet unless you are keen beach-trippers you'd be hard pressed to show that you had missed out on anything by choosing the less familiar region.

You may have to sign an inventory before taking possession. If so, check carefully before you sign that everything on the list is there. (See Chapter 5, WELCOME TO FRANCE.)

GITES RURAUX

France is the easiest country in the world for finding acceptable self-catering accommodation, largely because of the Gîtes de France organization. *Gîtes ruraux* are not the only self-catering accommodation available in France – far from it – but there is such a vast number of them all over France (about 40,000) that they exert an influence, in standards and in rent, over almost the whole short-let 'holiday' market.

To be officially listed and approved by the Gîtes de France inspectors, the holiday accommodation can be a small house or part of a bigger one, but it must meet certain standards. It has to have an independent lockable front door, proper cooking facilities, hot water, a bath or at least a shower, a proper sit-down flush lavatory, a fridge, and more. It is inspected and graded in terms of comfort and other features (architectural attractiveness, location, view and suchlike), and its rent has to be approved as reasonable for its size and grade. If it conforms, details of the *gîte* can appear in the annual booklet published for each *département* (county) of France, and the roundel '*Gîte Rural*' (literally, 'rustic shelter') can be fixed to the outside. Complaints lead to investigation by the authorities in the *département*. *Gîtes* that turn out to be unsatisfactory are struck off, although nothing prevents the owner from letting his property as a private venture, instead of as an approved *gîte rural*.

Rents are lowish, from £90 to £150 a week in 1990 for a *gîte* housing four to six people, depending on grade and time of year. This happy state of affairs arises partly because there is quite a lot of property in country districts that would otherwise be vacant (agriculture employs more tractors these days, but fewer people) and partly because owners can get useful tax concessions and loans if they agree to refurbish cottages and to reserve them for holiday letting for a number of years – an official policy aimed at stimulating rural life. So a farmer who moves into a modern villa on the outskirts of his village will probably keep possession of his ancestral cottage on the village square, turning it into a *gîte rural* if it can be made to meet the standards. This will bring in some money during the holiday season, and fulfill the traditional French desire to keep savings in *la pierre* (stone, i.e. property) as well as in *l'or* (gold) rather than in bits of paper.

OTHER TYPES OF ACCOMMODATION

Apart from *gîtes ruraux*, there are lots of holiday cottages and other buildings on offer in country districts. They're not *gîtes ruraux* either because they don't meet the standards or because they are way above them, with swimming-pools, helicopter pads and gold-plated taps. The rents, of course, will in consequence be lower or higher than the average *gîte rural* rent.

There are almost no *gîtes ruraux* on the coast. Indeed, the point of the organization is to improve country life (and help farmers, villages, grocers and bakers), rather than to add to the commercial activity in seaside resorts. But seaside resorts do have a lot of self-catering accommodation, some of it in purpose-built blocks. The sea has spawned a great deal of newer property, most of which is in the form of apartments. Unless you pay a lot of money, the facilities are usually still quite basic, and modern French building leaves a lot to be desired in terms of such things as noise insulation. Such places fetch higher rents than *gîtes ruraux*, but not vastly higher, for accommodation of equivalent comfort, otherwise canny French families might decide to go inland instead, and do their swimming in a river or a lake.

Finally, there are short-let places in towns, including Paris, although as these are not what the normal French person would choose for a holiday, they are not influenced by *gîte rural* standards. For more details of all types of properties, contact the companies listed in Chapter 3.

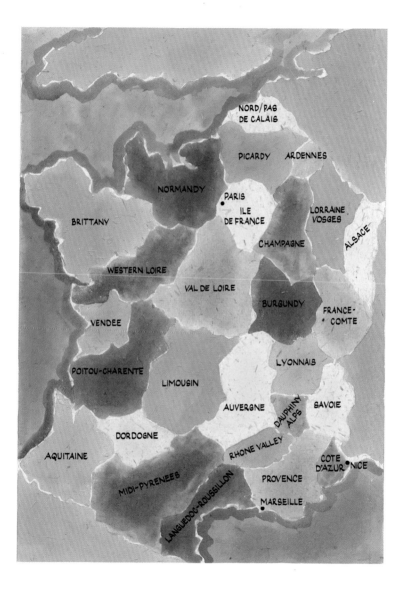

WHAT WILL IT COST?

Self-catering compares favourably with other kinds of holiday in respect of cost. In fact, for some people it's the only kind of holiday that is financially viable.

Let's assume that you will take the car, like the vast majority of self-caterers. For any sort of holiday in France, your 'overheads' will include:

- modest health insurance (see Chapter 4, GETTING READY).
- extra car insurance (to include flying out spare parts unless you have a Renault, Citroën or Peugeot).
- cross-Channel fares (see Chapter 3, MAKING PLANS)
- petrol: to be safe, allow for it to cost 20% more in France. If you plan to use French motorways (*autoroutes à péage*), allow about 30 centimes extra per km, or 5p per mile, for the toll (see Chapter 3, MAKING PLANS).
- hotels *en route*. On the whole, these are cheaper than in Britain. You can get a decent room for two at simple places of the 'Logis de France' type for 250F or less (1990 prices), and a cot or child's bed may be available at a small extra charge.
- a 'cushion' of extra money for emergencies. Cars break down; doctors and chemists have to be paid in cash (it's when you're back home that you'll get your money back, or some of it). If you break the law on the road (speeding; neglecting seat belts; going through a red light), you may get away with a mere 300F on-the-spot fine – or it may cost you a lot more (see Chapter 11, DRIVING).
- a 'cushion' for temptations.
- pocket money.
- money for food, drink and housekeeping.

SELF-CATERING

Now for the specific self-catering cost. For a basic country house with few amenities (such as the one described in WHAT WILL IT BE LIKE?, this chapter) sleeping four to six people, expect to pay between around £120 per week. It will be less than this if the house is very remote, and more if it is newly decorated or recently modernized. Add on 10% to 20% if a pretty garden and such items as sunbeds are provided. Add on up to 50% if the house is in, or within easy reach of, an attractive centre, and more than that if the centre is one of high tourist interest, such as Lourdes or Aix-en-Provence. Expect to pay double if the property is by the sea, especially in the south. And the extreme south-west, around Biarritz, and the Côte d'Azur are special cases.

Modern property is usually more expensive to hire than older, restored property, wherever it is, perhaps to the order of around 20%. At one extreme you have the Côte d'Azur villa, with pool, gardens, maid and laundry service, nicely but simply appointed, and with a kitchen which looks good but, when you inspect it, reveals the assumption that the residents will eat out every night. This can cost as much as £2,500 per week. Ridiculous, but true. A small, modern house on an estate within striking distance of the sea at St Tropez, with no garden to speak of and three bedrooms, will be £500 a week or more.

You don't have to pay these outrageous sums, but the Côte d'Azur is not the only stretch of coastline. Some of the purpose-built resorts on the western Mediterranean are much less expensive than this, but most people would agree that the region is much less attractive too. The Atlantic coast is a much better bet from the point of view of cost, especially the further north you go from Biarritz, but there the climate is not quite so reliable for sunworshippers.

Interestingly enough, you don't have to travel very far inland for prices to dip substantially, and this way you might be able to get the best of both worlds. A final warning, however: the most popular seaside resorts have major traffic problems, and you may find yourself sitting in the car for quite long periods on your way to the beach and home again in the evening.

There are package deals available from the Gîtes de France

London office, Brittany Ferries and others, covering rent, cross-Channel fares and a hotel night *en route* where necessary (see the list UK-BASED COMPANIES in Chapter 3). Otherwise, the prices quoted here for self-catering accommodation are usually all-inclusive, which is to say that your own added expenses are simply those already mentioned. When this is taken into account, and other factors such as the complete freedom to come and go when you please, not to mention the attraction of having a solid roof over your head, especially if you have children, then the advantages of self-catering holidays are obvious.

THE ALTERNATIVES

HOTELS

How do these self-catering costs compare with staying in hotels? For just a couple travelling by car, there's not a lot in it if they're content with one- or two-star hotels. In 1990 you could get a double room with bath or shower and lavatory *en suite* for under 200F in small towns. That's a shade more than the nightly cost of a *gîte rural*. But you usually have to take a *gîte* for a fortnight, and you are almost certainly paying for room for more than two people. The travelling couple using hotels don't need to stay put. They might find that a worthwhile advantage. On the other hand, they can't do their own cooking and washing-up. Two hotel breakfasts, two restaurant lunches and two restaurant dinners per day add up to a tidy total.

Half-*pension* terms (breakfast and dinner at the hotel and a picnic at lunchtime) reduce the cost, but then you lose the glorious freedom of going around reading restaurant menus (which are always exhibited outside, with the prices) and making gastronomic discoveries. With your own *gîte*, you can have a colossal restaurant lunch and then a leaf of lettuce and an Alka-Seltzer, or a plain boiled egg, in the evening. If you're a bigger party, then self-catering will turn out much cheaper than hotels.

21

Chambre d'hôte means a room in the host's own home, and this arrangement is popular with many travellers. A substantial number of British people have themselves moved to France to run this kind of operation, and the standards tend to be high. In country towns and in the country itself, where the cost of buying property in the first place is not high, you can pay as little as 150F for a double room, including breakfast. Quite a few hosts are master chefs. If you stay in their homes you are usually expected to dine there too, and in such cases the room can cost as little as 90F, but the dinner will cost perhaps twice as much. It will probably be magnificent though.

CAMPING

As for camping, the first investment is obviously in the tent, and the second in the furniture, lighting, cooking and other equipment you need to take with you. French campsites vary in quality as they do anywhere else, but a great many are run by local authorities and fulfil certain basic standards. Others are indicated by signs saying something like *camping à la ferme* (camping on the farm) or *camping du lac* (camping by the lake), where there may be little more than a few electric sockets and a toilet block. These can be found through specialist brochures and amount to self-catering under canvas, although, like all self-caterers but unlike most campers, you can't simply move on when the whim takes you. In many areas, especially by the sea, sites may be of the ready set up kind, where the tent or the caravan is already there and you simply move in.

If you already own a tent and all the paraphernalia, camping in France will cost less than renting an average *gîte*. But not very much less, because all the expenses other than rent remain unchanged. The cost range of campsites is very wide, as little as 25F per night for a one- or two-person tent on the most basic site, or up to 100F or more for a more sophisticated multi-person tent on a pleasant site with good washing and shopping facilities. A very luxurious campsite can cost a party of four or more almost as much as a simple 'official' *gîte rural*, because on a campsite there is a charge per head as well as for the pitch. It's a matter of personal preference: the freedom to pull up your tent pegs and move on whenever the fancy takes you versus the private bathroom and the proper kitchen and fridge; the international friend-ships of the campsite versus privacy plus the chance of getting to know people who aren't holiday-makers but are leading normal working lives.

WHAT WILL IT BE LIKE?

France is full of little stone cottages, and many of them have been turned into holiday properties. If you are renting in rural France, this is almost certainly the kind of place you will get. It may be isolated, perhaps situated on a little road which, beyond the house itself, becomes nothing more than a farmer's track. Or it may be in a village. Surrounded by local people, you will be able to do your shopping in the village's own shops, or, where there are none (increasingly common, sadly) with the travelling baker, butcher or fishmonger, who announces his arrival by blowing the horn or ringing a bell.

The area of France you decide on is more likely to be governed by such considerations as the weather, how close you are to the sea and the length of the journey than it is by whether or not there is a particular kind of property available in the region. In any case, the variety of properties available, not to mention any variation in quality, depends less on where it is than on what it costs and the kind of locality it's in. If you go to a major centre, or a centre which caters heavily for the tourist trade, the standard of accommodation for the same money will be different, in the main, from that in a less popular region.

The first rule is that you get what you pay for. Having said that, you then bear in mind that the ratio between price and quality in French self-catering properties tends to be excellent. In other words, considering their quality, these properties are usually on the cheap side. This does not apply on the Côte d'Azur, where the enormous capital outlay required to buy the property in the first place more than justifies, at least in the owner's mind, the huge rents charged.

Let's take a middle-grade *gîte rural* as the norm. This is a fairly safe guide. There are so many *gîtes ruraux* all over France, and their average standard is so well known to all French people who rent holiday accommodation, that they measure other sorts of short-let places by that standard. They will pay more for that standard if the place is in a coastal resort, or in a town, or has special attractions (a private pool, for example). If the rent is lower than the normal *gîte* rent, you can expect the place to fall short of the standard in one way or another.

In all *gîtes ruraux* in any of the three grades there will be: an independent, lockable front door, so that you can come and go as you wish, and adequate but not luxurious furniture. You will be very unlucky indeed if the property is not immaculately clean when you arrive. You will have established how many rooms and beds there are before booking. The bedrooms themselves will be quite small, as will the windows, especially in the south where the summers are extremely hot. The windows will have shutters, and the house is kept cool during the day by closing the shutters as soon as the sun is up and leaving them shut until the sun is low in the sky. The thick stone walls also contribute to a cool interior. There will be no carpets on the floors, though there may be small rugs here and there. The floors themselves will be tiles, either terracotta or ceramic, and this can apply equally to upstairs as well as down. When the upstairs is tiled the weight of the tiles on the suspended wooden floor causes the beams and joists to droop alarmingly. The French don't worry about this and neither should you.

You're usually supposed to bring your own sheets and towels, but there will be proper beds with proper mattresses and blankets for most members of your party, though if you are filling the place to the maximum of its advertised capacity, one of the beds might be a convertible sofa in the living-room (this should be made clear in the published details). French pillows don't always appeal. Double beds often have one long, round bolster, and these can be very hard and uncomfortable. You will probably find some smaller, more comfortable pillows in the cupboards.

You'll get a bathroom or shower room with hot and cold water. The bathroom will be small, simple and functional. There may be a bidet. Even affluent French people don't always see any point in having more than one bathroom, and even if the property is designed to sleep two families, two bathrooms is very unlikely. There may be a second, separate WC. Or there may not. The French do like adequate hot water, although the system for heating it may be a little hit and miss. If there is an electric immersion heater you should have no problems, but remember that they are usually set to work only on cheap rate electricity, usually at night, with a booster period in the afternoon. This can mean that if you use all the hot water in the morning you will have no more for several hours. Otherwise you may have a gas system that heats the water as it runs through the tap, and these sometimes require a bit of skill to operate. Lighting the pilot light in the first place can call for nerves of steel, but once lit they work well enough. All the same, you have to make sure that the water runs from the taps at exactly the right speed. Too fast and the water runs cold, too slow and the gas goes out. The house may well not be supplied with mains gas, in which case the water heater (and almost certainly the cooker) will run on bottled gas. A spare, full bottle should be available in case either one runs out. You may need to have this explained to you when you arrive. (See Chapter 10, PRACTICAL HOUSEKEEPING, for how to go about this.)

The living-room and kitchen may well be open plan, which is one way of saying that they are the same room. This is a common arrangement in many French rural homes, where separate, more formal salons do exist, but are not much used from day to day. The rural French seem to manage very well without easy chairs, and you will have to as well. This is no hardship in practice; you'll be surprised how little time you spend sitting down (whatever resolutions you may have made about your holiday) and most of your sitting time will probably be round a table. If there's a garden, there may also be a table outside, placed under a tree for shade in the hottest part of the day. The pleasure of eating outside is so important a part of French life that you may feel it's worth checking before you go that this most essential feature will be provided.

Many people are astonished at how much garden they get for the money. In fact, this is not so surprising, as land is very cheap over most of France, and since there is no shortage of housing, neither is there any need to sell off land to build houses on. As a result, even the most modest properties often sit on plots of land that are enormous by British standards. But don't expect beautifully tended lawns and flowerbeds. It's more likely to be a patch of grass interspersed with trees – wonderful for children who need to let off steam.

The kitchen will be equipped to satisfy an exacting French person, although it may seem functional to you. Cutlery and crockery will be plain and simple, probably odds and ends from several sets that have remained in the owner's family for generations, only to be pressed into service for this latest business venture. Adequate crockery and cutlery should be provided, and it's very unlikely that it won't be. But if you do need any more, a knife is *un couteau*, a fork, *une fourchette*, a spoon, *une cuillère*, a plate, *une assiette*, and a bowl, *un bol*. As for cooking utensils, many French cooks seem to get by with remarkably few, but there should be all the pots and pans one can think of, plus gadgets such as tin-openers, corkscrews and so on. And proper coffee-making equipment, often including a coffee-grinder. Perhaps no teapot, though, unless there has been a series of British families bewailing its absence. Most of the French drink tea only when they are ill.

The French rarely use kettles, preferring to boil water in a saucepan instead, so it's unlikely you'll get one. You'll get a cooker, but the ovens in French gas cookers often seem rather fierce, so until you are used to it, set the thermostat lower than you would at home and watch the food like a hawk. There'll also be a fridge, but no dishwasher, washing machine or tumble dryer. There may be a vacuum cleaner, which you should make good use of before you leave.

The essential feature of this kind of property is basic simplicity, but it will also be pleasant and clean. Many visitors report an extraordinarily warm welcome from the owners. If the house belongs to a wine producer, you may find a couple of bottles cooling in the fridge to welcome you. And leave the house carefully in the morning, in case four or five fresh eggs have been quietly left on the doorstep, or even a few potatoes or courgettes, freshly lifted from the soil in the early hours.

In British-owned properties the equipment and fittings are generally of a higher standard. The houses may be a little more expensive, though not necessarily, since they must attract the same visitors as the French-owned houses do. But the kitchen, in particular, will probably be better equipped. The atmosphere of the house will be quite different from a French-owned one, and you must decide beforehand if that is what you want.

On the coast things can be quite different. In the north, especially in Brittany, you are likely to find small fishermen's cottages which will be of a similar standard, though naturally the architecture varies according to the region. In the south, the coastal regions have been much more heavily exploited for tourists, and there is much more new property to rent. You can expect to pay a lot of money in areas like the Côte d'Azur; the quality properties are quite breathtaking, but very expensive indeed.

The Atlantic coast, from Biarritz and north to La Rochelle, is very attractive. The southern end is still fashionable, if a little faded, but expensive. If you search carefully you can find properties with character in this region, but you will pay for them. Things should become less expensive the further north you go.

Between these two, geographically speaking, is the Mediterranean coast from the Spanish border north to the Carmargue. Much of this is made up of new resorts such as Port-Leucate and La Grande Motte, purpose-built on reclaimed lagoons that were once mosquito-ridden. This sounds unattractive, but they have been carefully done by the standards of such developments elsewhere.

WHAT ABOUT CHILDREN AND BABIES?

For many people, the most important consideration in planning a holiday will be their children. Some questions have to be answered even before you can decide what kind of holiday you want. What special needs do the children have? Are they likely to be satisfied? What about laundry facilities? Do I need a cot? Organized or supervised play? Babysitters?

On the whole, self-catering is the ideal choice for people with children. Its first and greatest advantage is, of course, freedom. This is something it shares with camping and, although most children find camping tremendous fun, parents usually find the extra comfort and convenience of a roof over their heads well worth any extra expense.

The freedom provided by both kinds of holiday is most valuable at mealtimes. In a hotel, however small, meals are taken only at certain times and in public or semi-public surroundings, so that a certain standard of behaviour is required. Now younger children and toddlers live their lives at a different pace from their elders – they don't want to sit and wait quietly for the pudding to arrive. French restaurant and hotel staff tend to be quite understanding and accommodating with children, because French people often take their children with them when they eat out. All the same, the freedom to sit at your own table, with no external requirements, is worth a lot.

Unless you and your children have exceptionally exotic tastes, you will be able to find everything you need for them in France. As with many topics in this book, the further you are away from urban centres or regions of high tourist population, the less choice you are likely to find in your shopping. This applies equally to such services as babysitting. You must consider this when planning where to go and what to take. If you are holidaying in deepest Brittany and you simply must have a certain brand of nappies, then you will have to take them with you. But be assured always that the French have children too, and though their way of life is different from ours in some respects, their everyday shopping needs are pretty much the same.

In any case, many people find that adapting their normal habits to fit in with what's available locally is an important part of the holiday. (When in Rome. . .) And once you know that you can find everything you need to make them perfectly comfortable and content, this should apply no less to your children than it does to yourself.

The greatest challenge in a self-catering holiday in France with children in tow can be getting there. Most British holiday travellers in France go by car. Leaving aside any driving on the British side, the journey from the Channel ports to the South of France or into Brittany is a tall order. Driving all day is a strain at the best of times, and it's particularly harrowing if the back seat is full of restless children. Some children are better travellers than others, of course, but if yours aren't too good, you can only try to minimize a problem to which there is no real solution. (A few ideas for this can be found in Chapter 9, the section on GETTING THERE.)

Above all, self-catering is probably the best choice for families on a limited budget. It can work very well indeed when two families holiday together, sharing not only the accommodation but also those chores – cooking, cleaning and washing up – that are the very things most of us want to get away from. The children are occupied with each other, and the parents can even escape from time to time, leaving the other pair on duty.

CHAPTER THREE

MAKING PLANS

Obviously, the two most important things to plan are the property and the travel. These are dealt with in this chapter, which includes a list of travel companies researched especially for this book.

FINDING A HOUSE OR APARTMENT

You may have a property in mind from the outset – one that has been recommended, for instance, or one that belongs to friends. If not, you have to start hunting.

Generally speaking, the earlier you book up the better, as the choice of property for the weeks you want will be better than at short notice. While it's not out of the question, especially in low season, to turn up somewhere and find a house on the spot, this can be a fairly risky plan of action either if children are involved or if the budget won't stretch to a few nights in a hotel, should they prove necessary.

You may start your search in your local travel agency, but a look through the weekend papers will usually reveal a host of small ads. Some are obviously for companies, others describe a specific property and give the owner's phone number (maybe in the UK, maybe in France). Some *appear* to be private, but are actually placed by companies. (This doesn't imply that the standard will be either better or worse.)

PRIVATE ADS

There's much to be said for booking direct with the owners – they should certainly know the property and the area, and be able to give quite detailed advice. If it's a house they use regularly themselves, you can be fairly confident that it will be well equipped (and you can ask them, of course – see also WHAT TO TAKE in Chapter 4).

Theoretically it should be less expensive to book direct with an owner – but you can only know for sure if you make a comparison with properties on offer from the travel firms.

Try to see photographs before you book, and ask for the names and phone numbers of a few 'satisfied customers' – the people you are renting from may *sound* wonderful, but you don't know them, after all.

You will probably be asked for a deposit of something like 25–40% of the total rental. Make sure this is all backed up in writing, and be clear about what happens if you need to cancel. It's usual to get a substantial portion of the deposit back if you cancel a couple of months before planned departure, and to forfeit the whole amount if you cancel at the last minute. Remember that travel insurance will often cover cancellation costs, so look into it as soon as you are about to part with any money. The main thing about booking independently like this is that you have to thrash out these details for yourself.

If you book privately, make sure the owners have property and contents insurance that cover any damage or breakages you or your party might make, and make sure, too, that their insurance covers you if the roof collapses on one of your party or in case any of you are injured by fire, for instance – this is very unlikely to happen, but it's essential to check. Better safe than sorry.

All of this applies if the owner is based in France, too. Take into account the cost of cross-Channel phone calls as all this gets arranged. . .

RENTING FROM FRIENDS

This is likely to be an informal procedure, without any deposits, etc. But check the position on insurance (see PRIVATE ADS, above).

HOME EXCHANGE

Another possibility is house-swopping, which can be arranged through an organization such as Intervac, which aims to promote international friendship. This gives you the opportunity to stay in a genuine French house, while the French spend their holiday in your home. The benefits are many – not least the fact that there is no rental to pay. Contact Hazel Nayar, Intervac Great Britain, 6 Siddals Lane, Allestree, Derby DE3 2DY; phone 0332 558931.

AGENCIES

A number of companies act as agents, putting owners and prospective tenants in touch. Gîtes de France is the official *gîtes* organization, supervised by the Fédération Nationale des Gîtes de France. Its London office has a couple of thousand properties on its books (see the company listing in this chapter). There are many more official *gîtes de France* listed in the tourist booklets of each *département*. While in France, you could have a look at some, for next year's booking.

Chez Nous is a family business that functions as an agency, with about 400 properties (see the company listing).

DIRECTORIES

The French Farm and Village Holiday Guide (Moorland Publishing) provides descriptions of holiday houses throughout France, with details of how to book them.

TRAVEL COMPANIES

Broadly speaking, the companies fall into three categories: first, there are the big travel firms that offer countless sorts of holidays to countless destinations, including self-catering holidays in France. They often have huge numbers of properties, and these may be handled on site on their behalf by small, local companies. Brochures from these firms are the ones travel agents are most likely to have, and booking can generally be arranged through a travel agent quite easily, as well as direct with the company.

At the other end of the scale are the independent firms, often quite tiny, specializing in houses in particular regions. A husband-and-wife team with 12 properties in one area of Provence, say, would be typical. These people are likely to know each house on their list quite well, and might be better than a big company in providing for special requests or needs – if they are given plenty of warning! You generally have to contact these firms direct.

In the middle come the medium-to-large independent operators who specialize in self-catering, with houses and apartments all over the country (and maybe in other countries too), often with 60 or 70 (though possibly several hundred) properties on their books. They tend to resemble either the big firms or the small specialists, depending on the size of their operation.

Our survey of some 75 firms that offer self-catering holidays in France showed that the price reflects the standard of the property rather than company size. You will probably find it most useful to get hold of brochures or information from several firms for the type of property, area and period you want, and to make a price comparison yourself.

Most of these companies offer to arrange travel for you. The big firms tend to expect you to arrange your flight or ferry through them, so they quote all-in prices, while the smaller ones tend to treat travel as an option. As so many people travel to France by car, companies almost universally offer ferry deals, but flights or fly/drive are usually avoided by small firms. (The specific information on travel comes later in this chapter, in TRAVEL OPTIONS.)

UK-BASED COMPANIES OFFERING SELF-CATERING HOLIDAYS IN FRANCE

We have tried to make this listing as comprehensive and as accurate as possible, and all the information in it was provided by the companies concerned. Inclusion in the list does not constitute a recommendation, nor are we suggesting that companies *not* included are unreliable.

As well as names and addresses, the listing includes telephone numbers and, in some cases, special phone numbers for ordering brochures – usually they have an answering machine taking brochure requests, which are dealt with very quickly. The directory also includes the regions of France where the companies operate, plus a short description of their type of business and the approximate number of properties on their books.

Many companies offer travel as well as accommodation (see the list for details). Give travel plenty of thought before making your booking (the options are discussed later in this chapter).

The listing also includes companies' registration with, or membership of, various bodies – ABTA, ATOL and AITO:

What is ABTA? The Association of British Travel Agents is a self-governing body that aims to ensure high standards of service and business practice from its members.

Tour operators and travel agents can be members of ABTA. Members should display their ABTA number on all brochures and advertising, and are required to adhere to a code of conduct, drawn up in association with the Office of Fair Trading, concerning brochure descriptions, advertising, booking conditions, etc.

Should an ABTA member go out of business, the Association will ensure that customers can continue their holiday as planned and return home, and will repay customers who have paid for holidays that have not yet started. In the event of you being dissatisfied with your holiday, ABTA has a conciliation and arbitration procedure for dealing with complaints.

You may therefore prefer to book your holiday through an ABTA travel agent or tour operator for added protection and peace of mind. For further details contact the Association of British Travel Agents (see USEFUL ADDRESSES at the end of the chapter).

What is ATOL? An Air Tours Operators Licence, ATOL, is issued by the Civil Aviation Authority and is a legal requirement for all tour operators who use charter flights (although it does not apply to scheduled flights).

The scheme provides protection for customers such that if the tour company fails, the CAA will ensure that customers on holiday can finish their trip and travel home as planned, and that people who have paid for a holiday that they have not yet taken will be reimbursed. You should look for the operator's ATOL number on brochures and advertisements to ensure that you qualify for this cover. For more information contact the Civil Aviation Authority (see USEFUL ADDRESSES at the end of the chapter).

What is AITO? The Association of Independent Tour Operators is an alliance of some 70 small tour companies, all specializing in a particular country or type of holiday. All members are fully bonded, either through ABTA, the Civil Aviation Authority, or by private arrangement with insurance companies or banks, so that your holiday is protected.

AA MOTORING HOLIDAYS
P.O. Box 100, Fanum House,
Halesowen, West Midlands B63 3BT
Phone 021 550 7401
Fax 021 585 5336
Automobile Association's tour operator specializing in self-drive motoring holidays in Europe for both members and non-members. ABTA ATOL
Approx 500 properties in: Paris/Ile de France, Aquitaine, Auvergne, Brittany, Burgundy, Languedoc-Roussillon, Nord/Pas de Calais, Picardy, Poitou-Charente, Provence, Rhône Valley, Côte d'Azur, Western Loire, Dordogne, Vendée.
Ferry Motorail

ALLEGRO HOLIDAYS
15a Church Street, Reigate, Surrey
RH2 0AA
Phone 0737 221323
Fax 0737 223590

Small, independent company. ABTA ATOL AITO
Properties in: Corsica.
Ferry Flight Car hire Fly/drive

ALLEZ FRANCE LIMITED
27 West Street, Storrington, West Sussex RH20 4DZ
Phone 0903 745793
Brochure line 0903 745319
Fax 0903 745044
Independent tour operator with ten years' experience in villa and cottage holidays. ABTA ATOL
Approx 600 properties in: Aquitaine, Auvergne, Brittany, Languedoc-Roussillon, Poitou-Charente, Provence, Rhône Valley, Côte d'Azur, Savoie and Dauphiny Alps, Loire Valley, Western Loire, Dordogne, Vendée.
Ferry Car hire Fly/drive Motorail

37

ANGEL TRAVEL
34 High Street, Borough Green,
Sevenoaks, Kent TN15 8BJ
Phone 0732 884109
Brochure line 0732 883868
Fax 0732 883221
Small privately owned company
specializing in self-catering holidays
with or without travel. Properties range
from simple *gîtes* and village houses to
luxury villas with pools. ABTA
Properties in: Paris/Ile de France,
Aquitaine, Brittany,
Champagne/Ardennes, Corsica,
Languedoc-Roussillon, Limousin,
Nord/Pas de Calais, Picardy, Poitou-
Charente, Provence, Côte d'Azur,
Western Loire.
Ferry Flight Car hire Fly/drive Motorail
Train + car hire

AQUITAINE HOLIDAYS
5 World's End Lane, Green Street
Green, Orpington, Kent BR6 6AA
Phone 0689 853366
Fax 0689 850931
Small business offering a wide range of
seaside villas and country cottages in
south-west France.
Approx 70 properties in: Aquitaine.
Ferry Car hire Fly/drive Motorail

AUTO PLAN HOLIDAYS LIMITED
Energy House, Lombard Street,
Lichfield, Staffordshire WS15 6DP
Phone 0543 257777
Fax 0543 415469
Family company specializing in self-
catering and self-drive holidays in
France.
Approx 90 properties in: Brittany,
Languedoc-Roussillon, Dordogne,
Vendée.
Ferry Flight Car hire Fly/drive Motorail

AVON EUROPE LIMITED
Lower Quinton, Stratford on Avon,
Warwickshire CV37 8SG
Phone 0789 720658
Brochure line 0789 720130
Fax 0789 720982
Small business specializing in villas and

apartments for families.
Approx 100 properties in: Aquitaine,
Brittany, Languedoc-Roussillon,
Limousin, Midi-Pyrénées, Provence,
Loire Valley, Western Loire, Dordogne,
Vendée.
Ferry Car hire Motorail

BCH VILLA FRANCE
15 Winchcombe Road, Frampton
Cotterell, Bristol
BS17 2AG
Phone 0454 772410
Fax 0454 774382
Family business specializing in travel-
inclusive self-catering holidays in France
with accommodation in *gîtes*, villas and
apartments.
Approx 150 properties in: Aquitaine,
Brittany, Dordogne, Vendée.
Ferry Motorail

**BEACH VILLAS HOLIDAYS
LIMITED**
8 Market Passage, Cambridge CB2 3QR
Phone 0223 311113
Brochure line 0223 350777
Fax 0223 313557
Family business offering villas and
apartments throughout Europe. ABTA
ATOL
Approx 160 properties in: Aquitaine,
Brittany, Languedoc-Roussillon,
Provence, Côte d'Azur, Loire Valley,
Dordogne.
Ferry Flight Car hire Fly/drive Motorail

BLAKES VILLAS
Wroxham, Norwich, Norfolk
NR12 8DH
Phone 0603 784141
Brochure line 0533 460606
Fax 0603 782871
Long established company offering a
range of self-catering holidays in
France. ABTA ATOL
Approx 360 properties in: Aquitaine,
Auvergne, Brittany, Burgundy,
Languedoc-Roussillon, Limousin,
Poitou-Charente, Provence, Rhône
Valley, Côte d'Azur, Savoie and
Dauphiny Alps, Loire Valley, Western

Loire, Ardèche, Dordogne, Vendée.
Ferry Fly/drive Motorail

BOWHILLS
Mayhill Farm, Mayhill Lane,
Swanmore, Southampton, Hampshire
SO3 2QW
Phone 0489 877627
Brochure line 0489 878567 ━
Fax 0489 877872

Family run company offering a wide
range of unusual properties, many with
pools. ATOL

Approx 260 properties in: Aquitaine,
Auvergne, Brittany, Languedoc-
Roussillon, Limousin, Midi-Pyrénées,
Poitou-Charente, Provence, Côte
d'Azur, Loire Valley, Western Loire,
Dordogne, Vendée.

Ferry Flight Car hire Fly/drive Motorail

BRITTANY CARAVAN HIRE
15 Winchcombe Road, Frampton
Cotterell, Bristol BS17 2AG
Phone 0454 772410
Fax 0454 774382

Small family business specializing in
travel-inclusive mobile home holidays in
France.

Approx 150 properties in: Aquitaine,
Brittany, Poitou-Charente, Western
Loire, Vendée.

Ferry

CARISMA HOLIDAYS LIMITED
Bethel House, Heronsgate Road,
Chorleywood, Hertfordshire WD3 5BB
Phone 09278 4235
Brochure line 09278 4236

Family business but the fifth largest
mobile home owners in France. Family
holiday specialist, all accommodation
leading on to private beaches.

Approx 300 properties in: Aquitaine,
Brittany.

Ferry

CHEZ NOUS
Netherley House, 85 Dobb Top Road,
Holmbridge, Huddersfield HD7 1QP
Phone 0484 684075
Brochure line 0484 682503 ━

Fax 0484 685852

Small family business offering privately
owned holiday properties, booked
directly with the owners.

Approx 400 properties in: Paris,
Aquitaine, Auvergne, Brittany,
Burgundy, Languedoc-Roussillon,
Limousin, Midi-Pyrénées, Nord/Pas de
Calais, Picardy, Poitou-Charente,
Provence, Rhône Valley, Côte d'Azur,
Savoie and Dauphiny Alps, Loire
Valley, Western Loire, Dordogne,
Vendée.

Ferry Motorail

CONTINENTAL HOLIDAYS
Eagle House, 58 Blythe Road, London
W14 OHA
Phone 071 371 1313
Fax 071 602 4165

Villa holiday specialists.

Approx 100 properties in: Provence,
Côte d'Azur.

Ferry Flight Car hire Fly/drive Motorail
Train + car hire

CORSICAN PLACES LIMITED
Great Beech, Battle, East Sussex
TN33 9QU
Phone 04246 4366
Fax 04246 4879

Medium-sized company specializing in
high quality villas and apartments.

Approx 40 properties in: Corsica.

Ferry Flight Car hire Fly/drive Motorail
Train + car hire

**COTTAGE RETREATS (VALLEE
DU LOT) LIMITED**
Abercastle, Nr. Haverfordwest,
Pembrokeshire SA62 5HJ
Phone 0348 837742
Fax 0348 837800

Small family business specializing in
restored period properties in peaceful
and spectacular locations.

Approx 25 properties in: Auvergne,
Midi-Pyrénées.

Ferry

CRESTA HOLIDAYS
Cresta House, 32 Victoria Street,
Altrincham, Cheshire WA14 1ET
Phone 0345 056511
Brochure line 061 927 7000
Fax 061 953 4444

Specialists in apartment accommodation
in France. ABTA ATOL

Approx 100 properties in: Aquitaine,
Brittany, Languedoc-Roussillon, Poitou-
Charente, Provence, Ardèche,
Dordogne, Vendée.

Ferry Flight Fly/drive

CV TRAVEL
43 Cadogan Street, London SW3 2PR
Phone 071 581 0851
Brochure line 071 589 0132
Fax 071 584 5229

Family business offering self-catering
properties, ranging from grand houses
to villas in the Côte d'Azur. ABTA
ATOL AITO

Approx 120 properties in: Côte d'Azur

Flight Car hire

**DAVID NEWMAN'S FRENCH
COLLECTION**
PO Box 733, 40 Upperton Road,
Eastbourne, Sussex BN21 4AW
Phone 0323 410347
Fax 0323 410347

Family business providing made to
measure holidays. ABTA

Properties in: Paris/Ile de France,
Aquitaine, Auvergne,
Alsace/Vosges/Lorraine, Brittany,
Burgundy, France-Comte, Languedoc-
Roussillon, Limousin, Midi-Pyrénées,
Nord/Pas de Calais, Picardy, Poitou-
Charente, Provence, Rhône Valley, Côte
d'Azur, Savoie and Dauphiny Alps,
Loire Valley, Western Loire, Dordogne,
Vendée.

Ferry

DESTINATION PROVENCE
3 Gallows Hill Lane, Abbots Langley,
Hertfordshire WD5 ODB
Phone 0923 262196
Fax 0923 30839

Specialists in holidays in the
Provence/Bandol area.

Approx 60 properties in: Provence.

Ferry Car hire Motorail Train + car
hire

DOMINIQUE'S VILLAS
13 Park House, 140 Battersea Park
Road, London SW11 4NB
Phone 071 738 8772
Fax 071 498 6014

Small company specializing in villas,
converted farmhouses and *châteaux*
(some divided into apartments). Most
properties have private or shared
swimming-pools.

Approx 150 properties in: Aquitaine,
Provence, Côte d'Azur, Loire Valley,
Western Loire, Dordogne, Vendée.

Ferry Motorail

ERIC TURRELL
Moore House, Moore Road, Bourton on
the Water, Cheltenham, Gloucestershire
GL54 2AZ
Phone 0451 20927

Small company offering a small number
of carefully selected properties.
Specialists in the Beaulieu sur Mer area.

Properties in: Côte d'Azur.

Ferry Car hire Motorail

EURO-EXPRESS
1 Charlwood Court, County Oak Way,
Crawley, West Sussex RH11 7XA
Phone 0293 511125
Fax 0293 511825

Medium-sized company specializing in
villas with pools in France. ABTA
ATOL

Properties in: Paris, Provence, Côte
d'Azur.

Car hire Fly/drive

EUROVILLAS (1967) LIMITED
36 East Street, Coggeshall, Essex
CO6 1SH
Phone 0376 561156

Small family business offering
self-catering holidays in less
commercialized areas of France.

Properties in: Brittany, Languedoc-

Roussillon, Provence, Côte d'Azur, Savoie and Dauphiny Alps.

Ferry Flight Car hire Fly/drive Motorail

FOUR SEASONS (LEISURE) LIMITED
Springfield, Bagley Lane, Parsley, Pudsey, West Yorkshire LS28 5LY
Phone 0532 564373
Brochure line 0532 564374
Fax 0532 555923

Small company specializing in caravan and mobile home holidays.

Approx 100 properties in: Brittany, Languedoc-Roussillon, Provence, Vendée, Normandy.

Ferry

FRENCH COUNTRY COTTAGES
Anglia House, Marina, Lowestoft, Suffolk NR32 1PZ
Phone 0502 589171
Brochure line 0502 517271
Fax 0502 500970

Small family business; every cottage is inspected by one of the directors. ABTA

Approx 550 properties in: Ile de France, Aquitaine, Auvergne, Brittany, Languedoc-Roussillon, Midi-Pyrénées, Picardy, Poitou-Charente, Provence, Rhône Valley, Côte d'Azur, Savoie, Loire Valley, Western Loire, Ardèche, Dordogne, Vendée.

Ferry Motorail

FRENCH COUNTRY HOLIDAYS
19 Churchill Way, Painswick, Stroud, Gloucestershire GL6 6RQ
Phone 0452 812685

Small family business specializing in houses and cottages in rural France.

Approx 60 properties in: Languedoc-Roussillon, Poitou-Charente, Provence, Rhône Valley, Loire Valley, Dordogne, Normandy.

Ferry Motorail

FRENCH LIFE MOTORING HOLIDAYS
26 Church Road, Horsforth, Leeds LS18 5LG

Phone 0532 390077
Fax 0532 584211

Offer flexible arrangements for a large range of accommodation (including camping and mobile homes) in France. ABTA

Approx 500 properties in: Paris/Ile de France, Aquitaine, Brittany, Burgundy, Languedoc-Roussillon, Nord/Pas de Calais, Picardy, Poitou-Charente, Provence, Côte d'Azur, Loire Valley, Western Loire, Ardèche, Dordogne, Vendée.

Ferry Flight Car hire Fly/drive

FRENCH VILLA CENTRE
175 Selsdon Park Road, South Croydon, Surrey CR2 8JJ
Phone 081 651 1231
Fax 081 651 4920

Medium-sized tour operator offering villas with pools, *gîtes* and apartments, also a selection of mobile homes in Brittany.

Approx 1000 properties in: Aquitaine, Brittany, Languedoc-Roussillon, Limousin, Poitou-Charente, Provence, Rhône Valley, Western Loire, Ardèche, Dordogne, Vendée.

Ferry Flight Car hire Fly/drive Motorail

GITES DE FRANCE LIMITED
178 Piccadilly, London W1V 9DB
Phone 071 493 3480
Fax 071 495 6417

Supervised by the non-profit making Fédération Nationale des Gîtes de France, which rents privately owned properties for self-catering holidays. Also offer French bed and breakfasts and family hotel accommodation. ABTA

Approx 2500 properties in: Paris/Ile de France, Aquitaine, Auvergne, Alsace/Vosges/Lorraine, Brittany, Burgundy, Champagne/Ardennes, France-Comte, Languedoc-Roussillon, Limousin, Midi-Pyrénées, Nord/Pas de Calais, Picardy, Poitou-Charente, Provence, Rhône Valley, Côte d'Azur, Savoie and Dauphiny Alps, Loire Valley, Western Loire, Ardèche, Dordogne, Vendée.

Ferry Fly/drive Motorail

HOLIDAY CHARENTE
Wardington, Banbury, Oxfordshire
OX17 1SA
Phone 0295 758282
Fax 0295 750900

Family business specializing in
houses/villas with and without pools in
the Poitou-Charente region of France.
Approx 20 properties in:
Poitou-Charente.

Ferry Flight Car hire Fly/drive Motorail
Train + car hire

**HOSEASONS HOLIDAYS ABROAD
LIMITED**
Sunway House, Lowestoft, Suffolk
NR32 3LT
Phone 0502 500555
Brochure line 0502 501501
Fax 0502 500532

Well known family holiday company
offering a wide range of cottages, *gîtes*
and bungalows in popular areas. ABTA
ATOL
Approx 450 properties in: Ile de France,
Aquitaine, Auvergne, Brittany,
Burgundy, France-Comte, Languedoc-
Roussillon, Picardy, Poitou-Charente,
Provence, Côte d'Azur, Loire Valley,
Ardèche, Dordogne, Vendée.

Ferry Flight Car hire Fly/drive Motorail
Train + car hire

HOVERSPEED LIMITED
International Hoverport, Marine
Parade, Dover, Kent CT17 9TG
Phone 0304 240101
Brochure line 0304 240202
Fax 0304 240099

Tour operating division of
cross-Channel transportation company.

Approx 60 properties in: Aquitaine,
Brittany, Languedoc-Roussillon,
Nord/Pas de Calais, Poitou-Charente,
Provence, Côte d'Azur, Savoie and
Dauphiny Alps, Western Loire,
Vendée.

Ferry

INTERNATIONAL CHAPTERS
102 St Johns Wood Terrace, London
NW8 6PL

Phone 071 722 9560
Fax 071 722 9140

Privately owned company offering
properties ranging from *châteaux* to
farmhouses and villas. ABTA
Approx 50 properties in: Paris,
Burgundy, Languedoc-Roussillon,
Poitou-Charente, Provence, Côte
d'Azur, Loire Valley, Dordogne.

Ferry Flight Car hire Fly/drive Motorail

JUST FRANCE
1 Belmont, Lansdown Road, Bath
BA1 5DZ
Phone 0225 446328
Brochure line 0225 448894
Fax 0225 444520

Offer a large selection of villas, *gîtes* and
apartments throughout France. ABTA
ATOL AITO
Approx 300 properties in: Aquitaine,
Brittany, Burgundy, Champagne,
Languedoc-Roussillon, Midi-Pyrénées,
Nord, Provence, Côte d'Azur, Savoie,
Loire Valley, Western Loire, Ardèche,
Dordogne, Vendée.

Ferry Fly/drive Motorail

KINGSLAND HOLIDAYS
1 Pounds Park, Plymouth PL3 4QP
Phone 0752 766822
Fax 0752 768464

Medium-sized company specializing in
high quality properties.

Approx 92 properties in: Auvergne,
Poitou-Charente, Provence, Rhône
Valley, Côte d'Azur, Ardèche,
Dordogne.

Ferry Motorail

LA FRANCE DES VILLAGES
Model Farm, Rattlesden, Bury St
Edmunds, Suffolk IP30 OSY
Phone 0449 737664
Brochure line 0449 737678
Fax 0449 737850

Small family business specializing in
self-catering holidays to the unspoilt
areas of France. Accommodation
includes *châteaux* and beautiful houses
with pools.

Approx 120 properties in: Aquitaine,

Auvergne, Burgundy, Champagne/
Ardennes, Limousin, Midi-Pyrénées,
Provence, Rhône Valley, Dordogne,
Normandy.

Ferry Motorail Train + car hire

LAGRANGE UK LIMITED
16–20 New Broadway, London
W5 2XA
Phone 081 579 7311
Fax 081 566 1395

UK branch of a European company
specializing in self-catering holidays in
France for motorists. Properties in all
coastal areas and Paris. ABTA

Approx 100 properties in: Paris/Ile de
France, Aquitaine, Brittany,
Languedoc-Roussillon, Poitou-
Charente, Provence, Côte d'Azur,
Western Loire, Vendée.

Ferry

LES PROPRIETAIRES DE L'OUEST
34 Middle Street, Portsmouth PO5 4BP
Phone 0705 755715
Fax 0705 812779

Small tour operator offering a large
range of self-catering holidays in
France.

Approx 90 properties in: Brittany,
Languedoc-Roussillon, Midi-Pyrénées,
Provence, Rhône Valley, Ardèche,
Dordogne, Vendée.

Ferry Motorail

MEON VILLA HOLIDAYS
Meon House, College Street,
Petersfield, Hampshire GU32 3JN
Phone 0730 66561
Fax 0730 68482

Medium-sized company offering a wide
range of self-catering holidays with
accommodation in villas (some with
pools), cottages and farmhouses. ABTA
ATOL

Approx 150 properties in: Brittany,
Burgundy, Corsica, Midi, Provence,
Côte d'Azur, Loire Valley, Dordogne.

Ferry Flight Car hire Fly/drive Motorail

MISS FRANCE HOLIDAYS
132 Anson Road, London NW2 6AP

Phone 081 452 7409/5901

Small family business specializing in
houses in selected regions of France.

Approx 80 properties in: Languedoc,
Provence, Côte d'Azur, Dordogne.

Ferry Motorail

NORMANDY COUNTRY HOLIDAYS
113 Sutton Road, Walsall, West
Midlands WS5 3AG
Phone 0922 20278

Specialist tour operator. ABTA

Approx 130 properties in: Normandy.

Ferry

NSS RIVIERA HOLIDAYS
199 Marlborough Avenue, Hull, North
Humberside HU5 3LG
Phone 0482 42240

Small, independent company offering
own design chalets, cottages and mobile
homes on a 4-star holiday village
complex with 2 pools, tennis courts,
restaurant, take-away and clean beaches.

Approx 28 properties in: Côte d'Azur.

Ferry

P&O EUROPEAN FERRIES (HOLIDAYS) LIMITED
Channel View Road, Dover,
Kent CT17 9TJ
Phone 0304 223000
Brochure line 0304 21442
Fax 0304 223223

Tour operating branch of P&O
European Ferries offering a variety of
motoring holidays. ABTA

Properties in: Aquitaine, Brittany,
Languedoc-Roussillon, Midi-Pyrénées,
Provence, Côte d'Azur, Vendée.

Ferry

PALMER & PARKER HOLIDAYS
63 Grosvenor Street, London W1X 0AJ
Phone 071 493 5725
Brochure line 0494 815411
Fax 0494 814184

Long-established company specializing
in large, privately owned villas and
châteaux with their own

swimming-pools. ABTA ATOL

Approx 45 properties in: Côte d'Azur, Loire Valley.

Ferry Flight Fly/drive

PIEDS-A-TERRE
Barker Chambers, Barker Road, Maidstone, Kent ME16 8SF
Phone 0622 688165/6
Fax 0622 671840

Company is an extension of Francophiles Limited, one of the leading agencies selling property in France. All the properties let have English owners but are typical of the area in which they are situated.

Approx 25 properties in: Brittany, Vendée, Normandy.

Ferry

RENDEZVOUS FRANCE
Holiday House, 19 Aylesbury Road, Wendover, Buckinghamshire HP22 6JG
Phone 0727 696040
Fax 0727 624576

Independent company offering a wide variety of traditional *gîtes*, cottages and modern villas in many regions of France. ABTA

Approx 250 properties in: Aquitaine, Alsace/Vosges, Brittany, Languedoc-Roussillon, Nord/Pas de Calais, Poitou-Charente, Provence, Côte d'Azur, Savoie and Dauphiny Alps, Loire Valley, Western Loire, Dordogne, Vendée.

Ferry Car hire Fly/drive Motorail

RICHARD CHAPMAN HOLIDAYS
Higher Bamham Farm, Launceston, Cornwall PL15 9LD
Phone 0566 772141

Family business offering mobile home holidays.

Approx 10 properties in: Poitou-Charente, Côte d'Azur.

Ferry Motorail

ROUSSILLON VACANCES
40a Broadwater Down, Tunbridge Wells, Kent TN2 5NX
Phone 0892 512005

Small independent company specializing in self-catering holidays in the Roussillon.

Approx 30 properties in: Languedoc-Roussillon.

Travel can be arranged through a registered agent if requested.

SALLY HOLIDAYS
81 Piccadilly, London WV1 9HF
Phone 071 355 2266
Fax 071 355 3008

Sister company of Sally Ferries, specializing in motoring holidays throughout Europe. ABTA ATOL AITO

Approx 80 properties in: Paris/Ile de France, Burgundy, Champagne/Ardennes, Nord/Pas de Calais, Picardy, Poitou-Charente, Provence, Rhône Valley, Côte d'Azur, Loire Valley, Ardèche.

Ferry Fly/drive

SBH FRANCE
Cavalier House, Tangmere, Chichester, West Sussex PO20 6HE
Phone 0243 773345
Brochure line 0243 533141
Fax 0243 533454

Family company offering a wide variety of property (including a *château*).

Approx 120 properties in: Aquitaine, Brittany, Burgundy, Poitou-Charente, Loire Valley, Western Loire, Dordogne, Vendée.

Ferry Motorail

SEALINK HOLIDAYS LIMITED
Charter House, Park Street, Ashford, Kent TN24 8EX
Phone 0233 647033
Brochure line 0233 646821
Fax 0233 623294

Tour operating branch of the ferry company. ABTA

Properties in: Paris/Ile de France, Aquitaine, Auvergne, Alsace/Vosges/ Lorraine, Brittany, Burgundy, Champagne/Ardennes, France-Comte, Languedoc-Roussillon, Limousin, Midi-Pyrénées, Nord/Pas de Calais,

Picardy, Poitou-Charente, Provence, Rhône Valley, Côte d'Azur, Savoie and Dauphiny Alps, Loire Valley, Western Loire, Dordogne, Vendée.

Ferry Car hire Motorail Train + car hire

SFV HOLIDAYS LIMITED
Summer House, Hernes Road, Summertown, Oxford OX2 7PU

Phone 0865 57738
Brochure line 0865 311331 ━━
Fax 0865 310682

Large tour operator offering a wide range of travel-inclusive, self-catering holidays in France. ATOL

Approx 500 properties in: Aquitaine, Brittany, Midi-Pyrénées, Poitou-Charente, Provence, Côte d'Azur, Western Loire, Dordogne, Vendée.

Ferry Flight Car hire Fly/drive Motorail Train + car hire

SLIPAWAY HOLIDAYS
Phyllis House, 2 Sompting Road, Worthing, Sussex BN14 9EP

Phone 0903 821000
Brochure line 0903 214211
Fax 0903 203157

Specialist tour operator offering a large selection of houses throughout France.

Approx 300 properties in: Aquitaine, Auvergne, Alsace/Vosges/Lorraine, Brittany, Languedoc-Roussillon, Limousin, Midi-Pyrénées, Poitou-Charante, Provence, Rhône Valley, Côte d'Azur, Savoie and Dauphiny Alps, Loire Valley, Western Loire, Ardèche, Dordogne, Vendée.

Ferry Flight Car hire Fly/drive Motorail

SPARROW HOLIDAYS
Hurcott, Oxford OX5 2RE

Phone 0867 33280
Brochure line 0867 33350
Fax 0867 33526

Family business offering self-catering holidays in mobile homes situated on well equipped campsites on the west coast of France.

Approx 80 properties in: Brittany, Vendée, Charente-Maritime.

Ferry

SUNROSE HOLIDAYS LIMITED
Longstone House, 30 Callington Road, Saltash, Cornwall PL12 6DY

Phone 0752 842616

Family business specializing in properties in the Pyrénées-Roussillon area.

Approx 100 properties in: Languedoc-Roussillon, Mediterranean Pyrénées.

Ferry Car hire Motorail

SUNVISTA HOLIDAYS
5a George Street, Warminster, Wiltshire BA12 8DA

Phone 0985 217373
Brochure line 0985 214666 ━━
Fax 0985 219874

Family business with personally selected properties in many regions of France. ABTA AITO

Approx 250 properties in: Brittany, Burgundy, Languedoc, Midi-Pyrénées, Côte d'Azur, Loire Valley, Western Loire, Dordogne, Vendée.

Ferry Motorail

THE VILLA COLLECTION
P.O. Box 391, 1 Martian Avenue, Hemel Hempstead, Hertfordshire HP2 5PR

Phone 0442 68667

Small company specializing in traditional French holiday homes.

Approx 250 properties in: Midi-Pyrénées, Côte d'Azur, Dordogne, Vendée.

Ferry Car hire Motorail

TUSSON PROPERTY LIMITED FRANCE
B.P. Ol Tusson, 16140 Aigre, Charente, France

Phone 010 33 45 31 17 36
Brochure line 0722 330021
Fax 010 33 45 30 32 11

Small family business offering self-catering holidays in traditional properties.

Approx 8 properties in:
Poitou-Charente.

No transport

UNIQUE HOLIDAYS LIMITED
117a London Road, Waterlooville,
Hampshire PO7 7DZ
Phone 0705 269331
Fax 0705 263873

Exclusive agents for Green Parc Ocean
holiday complex in Moliets-Landes.
ATOL

Approx 80 properties in: Aquitaine

Flight Car hire Fly/drive

VACANCES EN CAMPAGNE
Bignor, Pulborough, West Sussex
RH20 1QD
Phone 07987 433
Brochure line 07987 411
Fax 07987 343

Self-catering specialist offering a wide
range of properties throughout France,
some with pools. ATOL

Approx 600 properties in: Paris/Ile de
France, Aquitaine, Auvergne,
Alsace/Vosges/Lorraine, Brittany,
Burgundy, Corsica, France-Comte,
Languedoc-Roussillon, Limousin, Midi-
Pyrénées, Picardy, Poitou-Charente,
Provence, Rhône Valley, Côte d'Azur,
Savoie and Dauphiny Alps, Loire
Valley, Western Loire, Ardèche,
Dordogne, Vendée.

Ferry Flight Car hire Fly/drive Motorail

VACANCES LIMITED
28 Gold Street, Saffron Walden, Essex
CB10 1EJ
Phone 0799 25101
Brochure line 0799 513715
Fax 0799 24897

Medium-sized tour operator offering
cottages and villas throughout France.

Approx 210 properties in: Aquitaine,

Auvergne, Brittany, Burgundy,
Languedoc-Roussillon, Midi-Pyrénées,
Poitou-Charente, Provence, Rhône
Valley, Côte d'Azur, Savoie and
Dauphiny Alps, Loire Valley, Western
Loire, Ardèche, Dordogne, Vendée.

Ferry Fly/drive Motorail

VACATIONS ABROAD LIMITED
30–32 Cross Street, London N1
Phone 071 359 3511
Brochure line 071 359 3500
Fax 071 359 3456

Small tour operator offering a range of
self-catering accommodation in France.
ABTA ATOL

Approx 25 properties in: Paris,
Aquitaine, Brittany, Languedoc-
Roussillon, Nord/Pas de Calais,
Provence, Côte d'Azur.

Ferry Flight Car hire Fly/drive Motorail

VFB HOLIDAYS LIMITED
Normandy House, High Street,
Cheltenham, Gloucestershire GL19 4NE
Phone 0242 526338
Brochure line 0242 580187
Fax 0242 570340

Medium-sized, independent tour
operator, pioneers in the UK of the *gîte*
concept, offering travel-inclusive
holidays in rural France. ATOL AITO

Approx 420 properties in: Paris/Ile de
France, Nord/Pas de Calais, Dauphiny
Alps.

Ferry Flight Car hire Fly/drive Motorail

WEATHERGODS LIMITED
16 Seaside Place, Aberdour, Fife
KY3 OTX
Phone 0383 860180

Family business specializing in houses
in the south-west of France.

Approx 60 properties in: Aquitaine.

Ferry Motorail

THE TRAVEL OPTIONS

Travelling to France from the UK, the main options are:
Taking your car – using ferry or hovercraft; *taking your car and using motorail* (including a sea crossing); *fly/drive* (i.e. with a hire car waiting at your destination); *train* (with sea crossing); *train plus car hire* (with sea crossing).

As you decide just how to travel you will no doubt be weighing up comfort/speed/stress etc. against cost. The main points to take into consideration are

- how far you live from the main ferry ports, and how far from the continental ports your destination lies
- how far you live from an airport
- how much holiday you have and how long you are prepared to spend travelling
- how far you are prepared to drive
- the number of people who can share driving
- the timing: French roads are packed on the first and last weekends of August, and during the weekend of their 15 August public holiday
- whether you want to treat the journey as part of the holiday or as a necessary evil
- whether you want/can afford to make overnight stops
- the size of the party (a full carload costs much the same to transport as a half-empty one)
- whether your party minds long sea crossings or flying
- whether flights are available in your budget range
- how unrestricted you want your luggage to be (i.e. do you need a carload of baby things or want to take the windsurfer?)

TAKING YOUR CAR – DISTANCE, ROUTE AND ATTITUDE

Are you going to be a dawdler or a dasher? Dawdlers make the journey a part of the holiday, acknowledging that there's plenty to see *en route* to or from their main holiday place. Dashers pile into the car and *drive*. It's quite common for members of a party to have differing attitudes to the drive, some being by nature dawdlers, while others are dashers, so compromises often have to be made. You could always dash one way and dawdle the other.

If you live in the Midlands or South of England, it's quite straightforward and quick to get to a Channel port and hop over to France. Crossings from the south-east corner of England (Dover, Ramsgate, etc.) are plentiful and fast (details of ferries appear below). From the West Country there are much longer crossings that deposit you in Brittany, ready for a holiday there or down the Atlantic coast. Travellers from South Wales can get down to the West Country ports fairly easily, too.

From the North, North Wales or Scotland there's a long and exhausting drive to the Channel ports before the drive on the other side of the Channel even starts. And while the prospect of a long drive may not sound too bad when there's a two-week holiday in which to get over it, think of the return journey . . . home late on Sunday and back to the old routine next day, probably.

At some stage, regardless of how many drivers you have, it's a good idea to stop for a rest and sleep. The most pleasant way is a relaxed stop at a small hotel with a good dinner and a comfortable bed. An alternative (which may appeal to dashers) is to plan in an overnight sea crossing such as on the Plymouth–Roscoff route. Dawdlers from the North might consider crossing from Hull to Hook of Holland overnight – it's a roundabout sort of route but could be the start of a lovely journey of two or three days down the Rhine to the Vosges or central France, or on through the Black Forest and Swiss/French Alps to land up in Provence/Côte d'Azur.

Dashing through France, you will inevitably use the *autoroutes*. Most of France's motorways are toll roads (*autoroutes à péage*). Prices per kilometre vary, and travelling from, for example, Calais to the south coast will cost between £30 and £40. This will be in addition to the cost of petrol. (Prices are per vehicle, not per number of passengers.)

MOTORAIL

The idea of Motorail is that you and your car make a substantial part of your journey by train. British Rail offer the service north of the Channel, while French Railways (SNCF) offer over 50 services from Paris and the north coast ports to destinations in central and southern France (as well as to other countries).

The main advantage of Motorail is that it takes a lot of the hassle out of long journeys on the continent with a car. You avoid long drives and traffic congestion and should arrive at your destination on time and relaxed. You also save on the petrol, motorway tolls and overnight stop expenses that accumulate on a long drive through France.

Motorail journeys are timed to take place overnight. No conventional accommodation is provided, so you pay for either a *couchette* or a sleeper compartment (*wagon-lits*). A *couchette* is a berth in a compartment – usually there are six people (in triple bunks that fold up to provide seating by day) in each, and you are supplied with a blanket and fresh linen. The compartment may be shared with other travellers (though a large enough party ought to get one to themselves) and is not segregated according to sex, so it's not normal to undress in a *couchette* compartment. (Having said that, it's best just to use your own discretion – a T-shirt and shorts is quite normal.) *Wagons-lits* are more expensive. They are less cramped, though, and many have washing facilities and you are guaranteed privacy. Many people sleep very well on trains and think this is a terrific way to travel. Light sleepers can find the whole thing miserable and exhausting – you can only know once you've tried it.

On some routes a buffet service is available, but it is advisable to check this before travelling. On all services a free continental breakfast is provided on arrival at your destination while your car is being unloaded. If you are booking your house through a travel company, you may find they will arrange Motorail for you (see the list above). Motorail can be booked directly with French Railways (SNCF) (see USEFUL

ADDRESSES at the end of the chapter), through P&O European Ferries and through Sealink. On some services there are special ferry prices for Motorail passengers.

FERRY SERVICES

FERRY SHIPS

Ships can be good fun on hot summer days when the decks are pleasant to sit out on or stroll around. Inside, the facilities and catering seem to vary enormously not only from one shipping line to another, but from ship to ship.

If you have a vehicle, once you've been waved up the ramp and have parked to the satisfaction of the loading staff, you have to get out of the car fairly quickly and go up to the passenger lounges by the nearest staircase. Remember the name or number of the staircase and your deck number, so that you can find your car later! You have to take with you anything you might need during the crossing, as you are not allowed back down to your vehicle until the ship docks at the other side.

With so many sets of identical-looking stairs it's easy to lose your bearings, so try to hang on to excited children (especially just after embarkation or before disembarkation, when everybody is milling around).

On short crossings there tends to be something of a stampede as people board and grab sets of seats or tables for their parties. On longer ones it is often necessary to reserve seating when you book. (This applies particularly at night.) Night-time accommodation usually consists of reclining chairs or cabins. Cabins tend to cost something like £20 for a couple, but each ship usually has a few 'luxury' ones at higher prices, that need to be booked well in advance. Standard cabins are usually well below the waterline, are small (as are the bunks), can be poorly ventilated, and tend to pulsate with the throb of the ship's engines. Once you've got used to them, however, you can get a reasonable night's sleep. Many people bed down for the night in a corner of one of the main lounges, and it's quite a good idea to settle children with a couple of blankets. If you want a cabin and haven't booked one, you can ask the purser as you board. (A cabin may be a good idea during the day if everyone is tired and, as they are less in demand, you may get a quite pleasant one.)

Facilities on board vary according to the length of the voyage, but there's always food, some sort of duty-free shop and money-changing facilities. Sometimes there are telephones. TV lounges are quite common, and on longer journeys you may find there's a small cinema on board. Some areas are no smoking.

Not all the ferries are ships, of course:

HOVERCRAFT

On several of the short routes (such as Dover–Calais) hovercraft cross the Channel in about 40–45 minutes. They carry cars, as well as passengers. They tend to be fairly noisy and to vibrate quite a lot – and even if you get a window seat the view is usually obliterated by spray. However, they halve the journey time (although you take just as long over check-in and customs clearance as in a ferry ship). Refreshments are usually offered (payment required) and a selection of duty-free goods is brought round.

JETFOIL

These aren't very useful for France as they only run Dover–Ostend at present and don't take cars, but they offer a very comfortable and fast ride, as you fly just above the waves.

SEACAT

These Australian vessels were introduced by Hoverspeed in the summer of 1990. They are rather exciting high-speed ferries that cut the crossing time from Portsmouth to Cherbourg by nearly half. They take cars.

The list below shows the ferry routes, the companies and the journey times. Actual departure times are not included as they vary from season to season. [S] Summer sailings only, [J] Jetfoil, [C] Seacat. Hovercraft are operated by Hoverspeed.

For further information contact the ferry companies (see USEFUL ADDRESSES at the end of the chapter).

From	To	Company	Duration (hours.min)
TO FRANCE			
Cork	Roscoff	Brittany Ferries	15
Dover	Boulogne	Hoverspeed	.45
Dover	Boulogne	P&O European Ferries	1.40
Dover	Calais	Hoverspeed	.45
Dover	Calais	P&O European Ferries	1.15
Dover	Calais	Sealink	1.30
Folkestone	Boulogne	Sealink	1.50
Newhaven	Dieppe	Sealink	4
Ramsgate	Dunkirk	Sally Lines	2.30
Rosslare	Cherbourg	Irish Ferries	17
Rosslare	Le Havre	Irish Ferries	23
Plymouth	Roscoff	Brittany Ferries	7
Poole	Cherbourg	Brittany Ferries	4.15 [S]
Portsmouth	Caen	Brittany Ferries	6
Portsmouth	Cherbourg	P&O European Ferries	4.45 [S]
Portsmouth	Cherbourg	Hoverspeed	2.40 [C]
Portsmouth	Le Havre	P&O European Ferries	5.45
Portsmouth	St Malo	Brittany Ferries	9

Depending on your starting point and destination, these may be useful, too:

From	To	Company	Duration
TO BELGIUM			
Dover	Ostend	P&O European Ferries	1.40 [J]

Dover	Ostend	P&O European Ferries	4
Dover	Zeebrugge	P&O European Ferries	4.30
Felixstowe	Zeebrugge	P&O European Ferries	5.45
Hull	Zeebrugge	North Sea Ferries	14.30

TO HOLLAND

Harwich	Hook of Holland	Sealink	6.30
Hull	Rotterdam	North Sea Ferries	14
Sheerness	Vlissingen	Olau Line	8

TO SPAIN

| Plymouth | Santander | Brittany Ferries | 24 |

TRAIN

If you are not taking a car, train travel could provide a good solution – and you could hire a car to use at your destination (see HIRING A CAR, later in this chapter). You could go all the way by train if you wish, but there's no reason why you shouldn't drive to the port in England, for instance, cross as foot passengers and then take the train from the French port, picking up a hire car at the station at the end of your rail journey. This sort of arrangement might need careful planning to make sure it worked financially. You wouldn't be able to take as much luggage as in a car, but that is probably no bad thing! Berths in a *couchette* or *wagon-lits* may be a good idea (see MOTORAIL, above).

Long-distance rail travel in France is now extremely fast, thanks to their high-speed TGV (*trains à grande vitesse*) network. The journey from Paris to Lyon, for instance, now takes just over two hours on one of these trains, and they give a beautifully smooth ride. You have to reserve seats if you are travelling on a TGV, but that can be done from home. A supplement may be payable.

Children under four go free on trains, and half-fare is payable for 4–12 year olds.

Some tour companies (see the listing) arrange rail travel or rail travel and car hire. But it's very easy to arrange this yourself. British Rail International (Victoria Station, London – see USEFUL ADDRESSES) can arrange ferry or hovercraft to anywhere in France, starting either in London or at a port. They also have a credit card booking service, so you can book and pay for international tickets over the phone, and simply pick them up on your way. Your own railway station may be able to arrange tickets for you, or advise. British Rail can also arrange tickets for journeys between certain French cities (such as Paris–Lyon), even if they are not part of a round trip to/from the UK.

French Railways (SNCF) (see USEFUL ADDRESSES) can provide information and tickets for all journeys. What is more, they should be able to advise on discounts for young people, for the over 65s, and for people staying away for several weeks and so on, which may well make the train option more worthwhile financially.

FLIGHTS

Although normal tickets on scheduled flights (allowing you to change departure dates and times after booking) are expensive, there are much better deals available if you book well in advance, or spend at least one Saturday night away, or plan to be away for at least a month. (In each of these cases you have to fix dates and times when you book, and they cannot be changed later.) Although airlines such as British Airways or Air France are the obvious ones to ask, you might find that a less well known operator offers flights from your local airport to one close to your destination. You can ask a travel agent or simply ring the airport. Flights can be booked through an agent or direct with the airline. You can sometimes do it over the phone if you have a credit card.

The other sort of flights are the charters, though on the whole this applies more to big holiday destinations in the sun than to France. They often work as follows: big tour companies charter a plane able to take, say, 150 passengers from Birmingham to Nice each Saturday through the summer, and to bring 150 back. It could be, though, that they end up with less than 150 holidaymakers, so sell flight-only deals to independent travellers to fill up the seats. Travel agents can usually find out about this and make bookings for you if you choose this option.

As a very rough guide, a standard air fare to a French city might cost about £150 return, a non-transferable one booked in advance may be £85 or so, while a charter could be anything between £65 and £85.

Scheduled flights do have some advantages: they seem to fare better than charters on those busy summer days when air traffic congestion causes hold-ups. They may depart and arrive at more sociable hours than charters. Remember that a 4 a.m. departure might mean a night in a hotel, or a special taxi ride – balance that against the possible extra expense of a scheduled flight.

Very cheap deals can sometimes be found in the back of the Sunday newspapers, from travel agents who sell tickets bought in bulk. While these may be tempting, it is advisable to check the details fully before sending any money, although they are probably quite above board.

It is very risky to rely on getting cheap, last-minute flights if you have already booked your accommodation for specific dates.

Travelling by air, you always have to pay for children, and usually for even quite tiny ones. However, this varies from airline to airline, so do check. Get an assurance, too, that the child gets a seat and does not have to sit on your lap. People with babies in carrycots are usually put in the seats with plenty of leg-room – but do ask. And find out, too, whether you can make a seat reservation as you book – this varies from airline to airline, too, and can depend on the type of ticket you have. Generally speaking, the assistance and facilities are better when planes are not too crowded, and worse on a fully booked flight.

Baggage is restricted on planes. It's usually 20kg (about 40lbs) which is more than most people can carry comfortably. If you are worried about exceeding your allowance, you're probably packing too much. Uncrowded flights are much less strict about allowances than full ones.

Other things to take into account when deciding whether or not to fly are the extra costs and the total journey time. It's worth investigating the practicalities of a 5.30 a.m. departure before you pay for it. Watch out, too, for the departure time at the other end – will you need a night in a hotel on your way back? It's worth looking into the expense of railway, taxi or car-parking. Don't ever park in the short-stay car park unless you're just dropping people off or picking them up – a fortnight in there would cost almost as much as your holiday. As far as time goes, although the flight itself may be a mere hour and a half, add up the time getting from home to the airport, hanging round at the airport, etc.

HIRING A CAR

If you wish to hire a car for your holiday it is a good idea to arrange this from home before you go as this is likely to be considerably cheaper than arranging it upon arrival. You can also be more sure about the exact terms and conditions of the rental agreement.

You may find that the company through which you book your accommodation also offers car hire. Alternatively, the large car-hire companies, as well as many other travel agents and tour operators, offer car hire abroad. It is advisable to shop around for the best deal as many of these firms offer special deals for holidaymakers, inclusive of local tax and insurance as well.

Be sure to specify special needs, such as child seats, when you arrange the hire, rather than when you arrive at your holiday destination.

If you do decide to arrange to hire a car when you get there, things are a bit more complicated. Check the terms of the rental very carefully. If it is not based on unlimited mileage, make sure that the car's current mileage is recorded on the booking form. You should also ensure that any damage to the vehicle is recorded, that you are fully insured and that the car contains all the necessary equipment (see TAKING YOUR CAR – THE PRACTICALITIES in Chapter 4).

MOUNTAIN PASSES

If you drive through the Alpine or Pyrenean regions, you are certain to use mountain passes. These are usually quite exciting, and most of the passes provide excellent views of the surrounding area, but many are on narrow roads and often have some tight, unguarded bends (caravans and trailers are sometimes prohibited).

When planning your route, it is a good idea to check the details of each pass that you will use. Some smaller ones are closed at night, and many are only open from mid June to September. Tolls are payable on some passes.

For further details about all this contact the tourist office or your motoring organization.

TUNNELS

An alternative to passes on some mountain ranges are tunnels. Again, it's best to check the details of tunnels you might use when you plan your route. They vary in length, some being as long as 15km (9 miles). The quality can vary, too – some are beautifully lit motorway-style tunnels, while others are still rough-hewn from the rock with dodgy lighting. Tolls may be payable – they vary and may be as much as £15 per vehicle.

Be careful to note any special driving regulations concerning, for example, speed limits and the use of sidelights. And if you're driving by day, remember to turn on your lights as you enter and turn them off after you emerge! If you're wearing light-sensitive sunglasses, they can take some time to adjust to the rapid change of light.

USEFUL ADDRESSES

Name	Address	Phone
Air France	158 New Bond Street London W1	071 499 9511
Association of British Travel Agents	55–57 Newman Street London W1	071 637 2444
Association of Independent Tour Operators	PO Box 180 Isleworth Middlesex TW7 7EA	081 569 8092
Automobile Association	Fanum House Basingstoke Hampshire RG21 2EA	0256 20123
British Airways	Heathrow Airport London TW6 2JA	081 759 5511
British Consulate	109 rue du Faubourg St-Honoré Paris 8^e	42.60.14.88
British Motorcyclists Federation	Jack Wiley House 129 Seaforth Avenue Motspur Park Surrey KT3 6JU	081 942 7914
British Rail International	Victoria Station London SW1V 1JT	enquiries: 071 834 2345 credit card: 071 828 0892
Brittany Ferries	Reservations Offices The Brittany Centre Wharf Road Portsmouth PL1 3EW	0705 827701
Civil Aviation Authority	ATOL Section CAA House 45–59 Kingsway London WC2B 6TE	071 832 5620

French Embassy	58 Knightsbridge London SW1 7JT	071 235 8080
French Government Tourist Office	178 Piccadilly London W1V 0AL	071 499 6911
French Railways (SNCF)	179 Piccadilly London W1	071 491 1573 motorail: 071 409 3518
Irish Ferries Limited	2–4 Miriam Row Dublin 2 Ireland	0001 610511
North Sea Ferries	King George Dock Hedon Road Hull North Humberside HU9 5QA	0482 795141
Olau Line Limited	Sheerness Kent ME12 1SN	0795 580010
P&O European Ferries	Dover Kent	0304 203388
Royal Automobile Club	130 St Albans Road Watford WD2 4AH	0923 33543
Royal Yachting Association	RYA House Romsey Road Eastleigh Hampshire SO5 4YA	0703 629962
Sally Ferries	The Argyll Centre York Street Ramsgate Kent CT11 9DS	0843 595522
Sealink UK Limited	Travel Centre Victoria Station London SW1V 1JT	071 828 1940
Thomas Cook Travel (enquiries)	5–7 Priestgate House Priestgate Peterborough PE1 1JF	081 889 7777

CHAPTER FOUR

GETTING READY

THINGS TO ORGANIZE

PASSPORTS

Check that passports are valid for the duration of your holiday. Once they are 16, children need their own passport; before then they can be included on one or both parents' passports (on both is best, just in case one of you needs to come home urgently, for instance).

The standard, 10-year passport, valid worldwide, costs £15. You can obtain application forms from main post offices; the form has to be countersigned by someone respectable who has known you for two years. You also need two photographs. Send the form, fee and photos to your nearest passport office. *Arrange passports early* – they can take ages, especially during the summer months.

A British visitor's passport costs £7.50. It is only valid for one year, so is an expensive option. Also, it is only valid for travel in western Europe (this may have been revised by the time you read this).

INSURANCE

You are strongly advised to take out travel insurance before you go abroad. Holiday insurance will generally cover the following: loss or damage to baggage, loss of money, personal liability, personal accident, departure delay, cancellation or curtailment, legal expenses and medical expenses (including return home in an emergency).

A particularly useful feature of some policies is a 24-hour

English-speaking helpline which can be contacted to organize emergency assistance for you.

If you're using a credit card to pay for your holiday you may be able to benefit from free travel insurance which is now offered by some credit and charge card companies. (Check with the company.)

If you book your self-catering accommodation through a UK company, they will probably offer travel insurance. Otherwise it can easily be arranged through travel agents, ferry companies, some airlines, banks, motoring organizations and insurance brokers and costs around £20 per person for a two-week holiday (with a 50% reduction for children). You can usually organize it on the spot.

Whatever the policy, make sure that it is adequate – at least £100,000 of medical cover in Europe, plus related expenses such as emergency dental treatment, ambulances and, if necessary, the cost of returning to the UK. Look out for exclusion clauses – for instance, some policies will not cover you if you are driving, pregnant or over 70 years of age – and check whether the clause about 'pre-existing illness or defects' might apply to you. If you're planning to go hang-gliding, rock-climbing or motorcycle-riding, check that you'll still be covered in the event of an accident.

Remember that in almost all cases where medical treatment is concerned, you will have to pay up front and reclaim costs from the insurance company. The same goes for car repairs or any other expenses, so keep all receipts. Where theft or loss is concerned, you always have to make a police report (or report to the airline if that's where the problem occurs). Ensure that you keep a copy of it for your insurance company. Generally you have to bear a proportion of the cost yourself – such as the first £15–20 of each claim. More information later in Chapter 12, EMERGENCIES.

FREE HEALTH CARE WITHIN THE EC – FORM E111

Within the European Community a reciprocal agreement allows people from other member countries *some* free medical treatment. For UK citizens this (sometimes complex) procedure is carried out via Form E111.

Getting the E111

Obtaining the E111 is now much less complicated than it used to be. Simply go to any post office (main post offices will be more likely to have them in stock than sub-post offices) and ask for the form. Fill it in and present it to the clerk together with some proof of your British citizenship, such as passport or NHS medical card – a driving licence may be acceptable. The clerk will then stamp the E111 and it will become valid immediately. You will need one for each adult in the party, but children under 16 get registered on a parent's form. Photocopies of the E111 should be accepted abroad, as well as the original.

What the E111 entitles you to

In France the arrangement entitles you to just the same healthcare that a French person would be given – but this does not include flying you home or other special treatment. However, it *does* include pre-existing defects, pregnancy-related illness, sporting accidents and more.

In general, like any French citizen, you pay cash to doctor, chemist or hospital, and then get about 75% back later (although less than 75% for medicine that's not strictly necessary but is classed as 'for comfort'). You get a complete refund in the case of something dramatically serious. In France, incidentally, failure to assist a person in danger (*non-assistance à une personne en danger*) is a punishable offence, so in serious cases no doctor will take the risk of leaving you while they check whether you can pay. However, a Form E111 certainly simplifies formalities, making you 'credit-worthy' on the spot.

Using the E111

In the case of a visit to or from the doctor where you obtain a prescription, you follow French procedure with your E111.

Pay the doctor, and get the usual form from her or him (*une feuille de soins*). Pay the pharmacist and fix the sticky labels from the packets or bottles of medicine in the appropriate place on the form. Ask the pharmacist for the address of the local *Caisse Primaire d'Assurance Maladie* (*Où se trouve la Caisse Primaire d'Assurance Maladie la plus proche?*). Fill in the rest of the doctor's form. At the end of your holiday, post that form (and any others you collect), with the prescriptions and your form E111, to the *Caisse Primaire*. A few moons later you should get a money order, sent to you back at home. As you can see, private travel insurance is simpler, but of course you still need to keep receipts and prescriptions to send to the insurance company.

Play it safe and take out comprehensive medical insurance as well.

INSURANCE FOR DRIVERS/CARS

In addition to personal and medical insurance, those driving abroad should take out adequate insurance to cover breakdown and recovery services when on the continent (see TAKING YOUR CAR, later in this chapter).

TRAVEL

Double-check bookings for accommodation, flights, ferries, trains, car-hire, etc., and make sure you have the correct times and dates. Check what is included in the price of the accommodation and confirm any requests for extra beds, etc., in writing. Any tickets or other travel documents should arrive a couple of weeks before you go.

Plan your route if you're driving and allow plenty of time to reach the port or train station if you have ferries and/or motorail booked. Ensure that you have all the necessary equipment and documentation for each country you'll be driving in (see TAKING YOUR CAR – THE PRACTICALITIES, later in the chapter).

or. . .

Plan your trip to the airport; if you're on a very early flight and live some distance from the airport you might prefer to stay somewhere nearby the night before. For those leaving their car at the airport, make sure you park in the right car park (the long rather than the short-stay one!).

Plan your trip from the airport to your accommodation; don't leave it to chance or you may be stranded – or have to take a taxi at vast expense.

Find out any luggage restrictions and pack accordingly.

Make a list of emergency phone numbers you might need while away and write an itinerary, together with dates and addresses/telephone numbers, to leave with a close friend or relative.

HOLIDAY MONEY

CURRENCY

The monetary unit is the *franc.* 1F = 100 *centimes*; £1 = approximately 10F.

Notes are issued for 20F, 50F, 100F, 200F and 500F. Coins are in denominations of ½F, 1F, 2F, 5F and 10F (watch out, there are two sizes of 10F coin) and 5, 10 and 20 *centimes*.

You will probably want to take money in several forms. Traditionally, travellers cheques have been the most popular way to carry funds on holiday, but use of credit cards and Eurocheques is now very easy, except in the most rural areas. So you can draw on your current account at home, or use a credit card, as easily in Biarritz as in Brighton (with travellers cheques, however, you are at least aware of the allocated funds being used up as the each one leaves the wallet).

The main points of the most popular alternatives are covered below:

CASH

Changing some money into foreign currency before you go will mean you won't have to search for a bank as soon as you arrive or resort to the poor rates and hefty commission charges of exchanges that operate outside banking hours. For the journey itself you will need enough for drinks and snacks – if you're driving on *autoroutes à péage*, you'll need cash for tolls. Also, you should also have means to pay any on-the-spot fines (almost 1000F for speeding!). Cash will be needed, too, to buy a few basics on arrival. Although it would be foolish to take all your holiday money as cash, it can be annoying to constantly be changing small amounts.

Most banks hold only limited amounts of foreign currencies, so it is safest to give them two or three days' notice of your requirements. They only give out notes, not coins. There are no restrictions on the amount of currency you're allowed to take into France, but you are required to declare exports of local currency amounting to over 12,000F.

TRAVELLERS CHEQUES

Travellers cheques are the most popular way of taking money abroad. They are simple, safe and, provided you take a well known brand (American Express, Thomas Cook, or from one of the big banks), are accepted almost everywhere. The cheques can be in any currency – if you take them in francs you only need worry about the exchange rate when you buy, rather than when you use them. You can buy travellers cheques at banks, building societies and travel agents; you may be able to get them on the spot but it's advisable to order in advance, allowing about a week as they may have to be ordered from another branch. Banks charge around 1% commission on their travellers cheques but you may find that the building society rates are lower. Whoever collects the travellers cheques has to sign them in front of the cashier. On holiday, they can then only be cashed or used by that signatory – not by partners, friends or grown-up children.

To cash travellers cheques on holiday you'll need your

passport as a means of identification – cashiers are always on the look-out for potential thieves. Shop around for the best place to exchange them as rates and commission charges vary; as a general rule avoid late-night exchanges and hotels and stick to banks, where your sterling will go further.

The main advantage of travellers cheques is their refund service; facilities vary from issuer to issuer but lost or stolen cheques can usually be replaced or refunded within a reasonable period of time. Remember to keep a separate note of the cheque numbers and the issuer's emergency telephone number. If disaster strikes, this will speed up the refund process. The disadvantage of travellers cheques is that you pay for them when you collect them, so the money leaves your account immediately, as cash would.

EUROCHEQUES

If you have a cheque account, you can order a book of Eurocheques and a Eurocheque guarantee card. These cheques can be used throughout Europe to buy goods or to obtain cash (although there's usually a transaction charge for the latter). Unlike UK cheques, Eurocheques have space to write in the name of the appropriate currency – so you can write a cheque in francs, pesetas, German marks or whatever, as well as in sterling. The cheque is converted into sterling at the rate of exchange prevailing on the day that the cheque is processed by your bank, and deducted from your account along with a small handling charge. Places that accept them often display a sticker (a pale blue and red *ec* on a white background).

Once written and supported by a guarantee card a Eurocheque cannot be stopped, so it is extremely important to keep cheques and card apart or you could be in for heavy losses if they are stolen together.

If you know the personal identity number (PIN) for your Eurocheque card you may also be able to get money from cash dispensers; again, look for the *ec*. The machines will guide you through the transaction in English; all you have to do is tap in your PIN and the amount of foreign currency you require.

Eurocheques are widely recognized in France and you should have no difficulty using them in restaurants and shops. You will also be able to draw money from banks and obtain cash from dispensers that display the symbol.

Eurocheques are provided free on request by most banks, although you'll probably be charged around £5 a year for the card. Try to order them well in advance as it may take a few weeks for the card and your PIN to reach you.

CREDIT CARDS

Credit and charge cards are a useful way of paying for goods and services on holiday and, provided you can afford to pay off the balance within the specified period, they also make financial good sense. The main limitation with credit cards is that you have to stick to your pre-set spending limit, although you may be able to get this raised for the duration of your holiday.

France has truly taken part in the credit card revolution with cards being widely accepted. The Visa card, known as the *Carte Bleue*, is almost universally recognized. Since 1989/90 Access cards have been accepted by Visa establishments, as well as ones displaying the Eurocard or Mastercard sign.

On the whole, you are likely to get a better rate of exchange with a credit card or charge card than with other forms of holiday money because the credit card issuer can afford to deal at more competitive rates than the individual. Another plus is that many of the major credit card/charge card issuers operate a guarantee service for anything paid for by the card. However, don't rely solely on your credit or charge card, especially in out-of-the-way places – and not for fuel, as many petrol stations still refuse them.

TAKING YOUR CAR –
THE PRACTICALITIES

DOCUMENTS

Driving licence You must be 18 or over and in possession of a full EC UK driving licence when driving in France. Drivers who have held their licence for less than one year must keep to a maximum speed of 90 km/h (about 52 mph) and display a '90' sign on the rear of the vehicle. Signs are available from most petrol stations in France.

Vehicle Registration document You must carry the original registration document of your vehicle. If the vehicle is not registered in your name, you should carry a letter from the owner giving you permission to drive. It is routine practice in many European countries for police, if they stop a car for any reason, to check the vehicle's papers as well as the driver's licence, and carrying the registration document in the car is obligatory.

Nationality plate You must display a GB nationality sticker on the rear of your vehicle. The oval sticker should be 17.5cm (7in) by 11.5cm (4½in) with black letters on a white background. Most insurance companies, motoring organizations and ferry companies will provide a free GB sticker.

Special note on boats It is advisable to obtain a Certificate of Registration if you are taking your boat abroad. Further details of the Certificate can be obtained from the Royal Yachting Association (see USEFUL ADDRESSES at the end of Chapter 3).

INSURANCE

Everyone driving in France must be insured. Your UK policy will provide overseas cover to satisfy the statutory minimum requirements in France. However, this is unlikely to match even third party cover in the UK – so no personal, damage,

fire or theft cover is included even if you have a fully comprehensive policy. It's best to give your insurers a ring to check their specific recommendations – it will probably be a Green Card.

Green Card Although Green Cards are not essential in France, it is strongly recommended that you take one. (If you are planning to drive into Andorra you *must* have one, and they are recommended for Italy and Spain, too.) Most insurance companies will issue a Green Card free of charge for a set period. In the event of an accident, this card will assist in proving that you are insured. It will also assist in extending the cover your UK policy provides in France.

Transit insurance Most car insurance provides cover for transit from UK ports. You will need to check the extent of the policy if you wish to travel on ferries outside the UK, such as to Corsica.

THE CAR

Get it serviced, and check tyres.

Headlights Your headlights should be converted for driving abroad by using either headlamp convertors or beam deflectors. Yellow headlights are normally compulsory in France, but foreign vehicles may keep their white headlights, so long as they have lamp deflectors.

Car telephones Many countries exercise control over the importation and use of car telephones. In France motorists are required to put a sticker on the phone detailing local restrictions. The phone will probably be useless anyway. For further details contact your phone network, a motoring organization or Tourist Office.

Extra equipment It is strongly recommended that you take the following equipment when driving in France. The items are available from large garages, accessory shops and motoring organizations:

- red warning triangle – this is compulsory in France unless the vehicle has hazard warning lights. However, it is strongly recommended as an accident may render the vehicle's electronics useless.

- spare bulb kit
- headlamp converter/deflector
- first aid kit
- left and right external mirror (the left-hand wing mirror is essential when driving on the right)
- fire extinguisher

HOLIDAY HEALTH

If you're already taking prescribed medicines, make sure you have enough to last the whole holiday. Take a copy of the prescription with you, just in case.

Your GP will be able to tell you whether you require any booster injections or vaccinations for the trip, will be able to prescribe any special medical supplies you'll need and will advise you on taking very young children abroad. If you or anyone in your family has a serious medical condition, ask your doctor to give you a note of explanation to carry with you. A note is important in the case of allergies, too, such as to penicillin. It's a good idea to try to carry a prescription for spectacles, too, just in case yours meet with an accident.

As far as teeth go, toothache and a hunt for a dentist can ruin a holiday, so if you're due for a check-up it's a good idea to have it before you go.

Most holiday ills are a result of over-exposure to the sun and unaccustomed food (see HEALTH, in Chapter 11). So buy and use plenty of high-factor suncream, and go easy on the gastronomy.

FIRST AID KIT

A good first aid kit is essential on holiday. When travelling, make sure you keep it to hand. A kit should include the following (you may find it more convenient to buy a ready-made kit and add other things to it yourself):

- adhesive plasters
- assorted bandages
- absorbent lint
- cotton wool
- antiseptic creams
- disinfectant
- calamine lotion/sunburn creams
- insect bite cream/repellent
- travel sickness tablets
- pain relief tablets, such as aspirin
- scissors
- safety pins
- tweezers
- thermometer
- any medicines prescribed by your GP

HAYFEVER

Acute sufferers will probably want to head for coastal regions where on-shore winds will disperse the local pollen. Even if you think you've found a pollen-free retreat, take medication with you as familiar brands may not be available.

If you'd like more information on how to plan a hayfever-free trip you can send for the *Holidays Without Hayfever Report*. Write to: Dr Jean Emberlin, Pollen Research Unit, Geography Department, Polytechnic of North London, 383 Holloway Road, London N7 8DB.

USEFUL ADDRESSES

The Department of Health's leaflet, *The Traveller's Guide To Health* (form T1), which includes further information about the E111 and claiming sickness benefits abroad, is available at post offices along with form E111. Alternatively you can write to: Health Publications Unit, No.2 Site, Heywood Stores, Manchester Road, Heywood, Lancashire, OL10 2PZ or phone free on 0800 555 777. People living in Northern Ireland should should write to the address below for information, advice or form E111: Department of Health and Social Services, Overseas Branch, Lindsay House, 8–14 Callender Street, Belfast BT1 5DP.

The following may be able to offer general advice on holiday health, including vaccinations: British Airways Travel Clinics (contact 071 831 5333 for details of your nearest clinic), MASTA – Medical Advisory Service for Travellers Abroad (071 631 4408), Trailfinders Medical Centre (071 938 3999) and Thomas Cook Medical Centre (071 408 4157).

AT HOME

- arrange for pets to be cared for while you're away
- cancel milk/papers
- unplug all electrical appliances
- deposit special valuables in the bank
- ask someone to keep an eye on your house, water the plants, remove visible mail, etc.
- inform the DSS that you're going abroad if you're receiving any form of benefit, as it may be affected.

WHAT TO TAKE

The lists below provide an average sort of checklist – they will inevitably be too long for some readers, too short for others. Take some of the items only if you are driving.

TRAVEL

- passports
- travel documents – e.g. tickets, insurance certificates
- money – travellers cheques, Eurocheques, credit cards etc. (make a note of numbers and keep them separately). Check credit card spending limits are sufficient if you're planning to use them while away, otherwise you may prefer to leave them at home.

HEALTH AND TOILETRIES

- prescriptions – for medicines, contact lenses, glasses
- first-aid kit – see HOLIDAY HEALTH, above
- travel sickness tablets
- contraception
- tampons
- contact lens solutions
- small mirror
- toiletries for yourself (or the whole family)
- insect repellent
- sun protection
- moist wipes

USEFUL SUNDRIES

- guide books/good phrase book
- back packs and/or money belts: useful for carrying maps and valuables once you're there.
- holiday reading
- radio/cassette player and cassettes
- camera/films
- plastic bags
- small sewing kit
- alarm clock
- torch – at least one if you're staying in the country
- adjustable spanner (you may need it for gas bottles)
- screwdriver (there may be one in the house but you'll know where yours is!)
- calculator (useful for converting currencies)
- scissors
- penknife
- string
- continental plug adaptor for electrical appliances
- roll of lavatory paper
- pen and paper
- plug-in mosquito device (Boots and similar stores) if you're heading for the south

LINEN

- sheets and pillowcases for everyone
- bath towels and towels for the beach
- teacloths

FOR BABIES AND YOUNG CHILDREN

- disposable nappies: but don't take supplies for the whole holiday – you'll be able to buy them when you get there!
- baby toiletries
- wipes
- bibs
- feeding cup/bottles (if your baby still needs a sterilized bottle you could take bottles with disposable, pre-sterilized liners/teats)
- jars of favourite baby food
- hat (with an all-round brim to shield the neck) or sun-shade
- high factor sun-protection cream (see HEALTH, Chapter 11)
- travel games
- toys
- wellington boots
- stick-on sun shade for the car (your own or a hire car)
- familiar bedding for very little ones

FOR THE KITCHEN

Your kitchen in France will probably have everything you need – and anything vital can always be bought. The following may prove useful, and you may use some items on the journey out:

- airtight containers
- vacuum flask
- cool bag (for picnics)
- plastic cups
- favourite sharp knife/potato peeler
- corkscrew/bottle opener
- tin-opener
- kitchen scissors
- measuring jug (calibrated in grams and ounces)

- safety matches
- foil/clingfilm
- a few plastic bags/dustbin bags

If you can't survive without them. . .

- egg cups
- tea pot/strainer
- pepper mill

FOOD

It's only worth taking food to cater for personal addictions – such as to tea, Marmite, marmalade, brown sauce or pickle (with *French* cheese?). See the sections on food in France.

CHAPTER FIVE

WELCOME TO FRANCE

The precise arrangements for arrival will be different from one house to another, and you should find out the procedure before you depart. Perhaps you will have to pick up keys from an office; maybe you will be met by an English agent or the *concierge* (caretaker); *Madame* or *Monsieur* (the owner) might be on site; or – just as likely – you may be on your own with no one to show you around.

INVENTORY

One of the things you will have to tackle is the inventory – you may be expecting to hand over a deposit at this stage, to be returned when you leave.

The vocabulary below should help with the inventory:

allume-gaz	gas-lighter
ampoule	electric light bulb
– *à baïonnette*	– with bayonet base
– *à vis*	– with screw base
assiette creuse	soup plate
assiette plate	dinner plate
balai	broom
balai éponge	squeezy mop
balance	household scales
bassin	basin
bassine	basin

batteur à oeufs	egg beater
beurrier	butter dish
boîte à pain	bread box
bol (à déjeuner)	bowl (not cup) for breakfast coffee
bouilloire	kettle
bouteille (or cylindre) de gaz	cooking gas bottle
broc	large jug
brochette	skewer
cafetière	coffee pot
carafe	decanter
casserole	saucepan
cendrier	ashtray
chiffon	duster, rag
cintre	coat-hanger
cocotte-minute	pressure-cooker
coquetier	egg-cup
corbeille à pain	bread basket
couperet	meat cleaver
couteau	knife
– de cuisine	kitchen knife
– à découper	carving knife
– à huîtres	oyster knife
couvercle	lid
couvert	set of knife, fork, spoon
couverture	blanket
cuiller, cuillère	spoon
cuisinière	cooker
cuvette	bowl, basin
débouchoir	rubber plunger
décapsuleur	crown cap bottle-opener
descente de lit	bedside mat
dessous de bouteille	bottle-mat, coaster
– de plat, d'assiette	table-mat
– de verre	coaster
drap	sheet

eau de javel	household disinfectant, bleach
écumoire	skimming ladle
édredon	eiderdown
égouttoir	drying-up rack; basket of deep-frier
entonnoir	funnel
épluche-légumes	vegetable peeler
éponge	sponge
essuie-vaisselle	drying-up towel
fait-tout	stew pan
fer à repasser	iron (laundry)
fouet à oeufs	egg whisk
gril	ridged plaque for heating on gas ring (for grilling steak)
grille-pain	toaster
hachoir	chopping knife
huilier	oil and vinegar cruet
lavette	saucepan brush, washing-up mop
lit	bed
– grand lit	double bed
– pour une personne	single bed
– pliant	folding bed
lits superposables	bunks
louche	ladle
marmite	stew pan
matelas	mattress
mazout	fuel oil as used for heaters with chimneys
moule à gâteaux	cake mould
moulin à café	coffee grinder
– à légumes	vegetable mill
oreiller	pillow
ouvre-boîte	tin opener
panier à bouteilles	bottle carrier
– à salade	salad shaker

papier hygénique (toilette)	toilet paper
passoire	strainer, colander
pelle	shovel, scoop
planche à découper	carving board
plat	dish
– à four (allant au four)	baking dish
plateau	tray
poêle	stove (room heater); frying pan
poivrier	pepper pot, mill
porte-balai	lavatory brush holder
porte-savon	soap dish
poubelle	dustbin
presse-citron	lemon squeezer
ramasse-couverts	cutlery tray
ramasse-miettes	crumb tray, crumb scoop
râpe-fromage	cheese grater
réchaud	boiling ring
rouleau à pâtisserie	rolling pin
saladier	salad bowl
salière	salt cellar
serviette-éponge	bath towel
soucoupe	saucer
soupière	soup tureen
tapis	carpet, mat
tasse	cup
théière	tea pot
tire-bouchon	corkscrew
torchon	floorcloth, dishcloth, duster
traversin	bolster
vaisselle	crockery
vase	vase
vase de nuit	chamber pot
verre	glass
verre gradué	graduated measure

THINGS TO ASK THE CONCIERGE/AGENT

If someone *is* there to show you what's what, they will most probably have a routine for showing how awkward equipment works – still, the chances are they will just have left as you discover that you only have one set of keys for six people, or some other inconvenience.

Therefore (though we're not suggesting that you ask all the questions below!) it may be worth having a quick run-through on the basics before the owner, *concierge* or agent disappears, or at any rate before nightfall. (The list and questions are given in English and French in case you need to ask in French.)

May we check a few things before you go, please?
Est-ce qu'on peut vérifier des choses pendant que vous êtes là?

Where can I park?
Où est-ce que je peux me garer?

How does this work, please?
Ceci fonctionne comment?

door/keys	*la porte, les clefs*
windows	*les fenêtres*
shutters	*les volets*
shower	*la douche*
oven	*le four*
washing machine	*la machine à laver*
lights	*les lampes*
telephone	*le téléphone*
water heater	*le chauffe-eau*
air conditioning	*la climatisation*

Could you let us have some more . . ., please?
Veuillez nous donner des . . . supplémentaires, s'il vous plaît?

keys	*clefs*
pillows	*oreillers*

sheets	*draps*
blankets/duvets	*couvertures*
towels (these may not be provided)	*serviettes*
lavatory paper	*papier toilette*
light bulbs	*ampoules*
coat hangers	*cintres*
cutlery	*couverts*
crockery	*vaisselle*
glasses	*verres*

Where should we put rubbish?
Où est-ce qu'il faut mettre les ordures?

Which way to the. . .?	*Où se trouve. . .*
Is it open tomorrow?	*C'est ouvert demain?*
supermarket/shop	*le supermarché/magasin*
baker	*la boulangerie*
bank/exchange	*la banque/change*
post office	*la poste*
petrol station	*la station service*
tourist office	*le syndicat d'initiative*
pharmacy	*la pharmacie*

Would you be able to arrange a babysitter for us?
Pourriez-vous nous chercher un baby-sitter?

Could us give us the name and address of a local doctor, please?
Avez-vous les coordonnées du médecin le plus proche, s'il vous plaît?

When does the cleaner come? (if applicable)
La femme de ménage vient quand?

Monday	*lundi*
Tuesday	*mardi*
Wednesday	*mercredi*
Thursday	*jeudi*
Friday	*vendredi*

Saturday	*samedi*
Sunday	*dimanche*
daily	*chaque jour/tous les jours*
morning/afternoon	*le matin/l'après-midi*

Where can we get in touch with you?
Où est-ce que nous pouvons vous joindre?

BASIC SHOPPING STRAIGHT AWAY

Though some houses come complete with a 'welcome pack' of basics to get you started, you will probably arrive to discover that the cupboards are bare, and might like to stock up on a few basics straight away. (You may have brought some of these with you, of course, especially if you have travelled by car). Most of the ideas on the list below will be found in the local supermarket or a general food shop, although fruit and salad will probably be better from the market, if you find one (see Chapter 7, SHOPPING FOR FOOD).

You may decide to eat out on your first evening, so the next day's breakfast will be your main concern. If you decide to cook in, you could refer to MENUS AND RECIPES where shopping lists are included.

mineral water	*eau minérale*
wine	*vin*
soft drinks	*boissons non alcoolisées*
orange juice	*jus d'orange*
milk	*lait*
tea	*thé*
coffee ground/instant	*café moulu/instantané*
beer	*bière*
butter	*beurre*
margarine	*margarine*
jam	*confiture*

bread (this is always available fresh in the morning, and usually on Sunday)	*pain*
breakfast cereal	*céréales, cornflakes*
cheese	*fromage*
eggs	*oeufs*
cold meat	*charcuterie*
salad	*salade*
vegetables	*légumes*
fruit	*fruits*
salt	*sel*
matches	*allumettes*
lavatory paper	*papier hygiénique*
washing up liquid	*liquide vaisselle*
local map	*carte de la région*
town plan	*plan de ville*

See Chapter 11, the section on SURVIVAL SHOPPING, if you discover that you have forgotten something vital.

CHAPTER SIX

EATING AND DRINKING

THE FRENCH DAY

The working day in France begins much earlier than in Britain. Most people are in the office by 8 a.m., having stopped off at a café on the way for breakfast (*le petit-déjeuner*) – usually a cup of coffee and a *croissant*. There's no break then until lunch (*le déjeuner*) at 12. This is the most important meal of the day, especially in the south, where the hot summer weather is an added incentive to stay put in the middle of the day. Normal French people have a 'lunch-hour' lasting two hours, and most small towns have several restaurants that are packed to the doors at lunch-time. These places are usually very informal, with little or no choice of menu, and some of them do not open in the evening. Most towns and villages throughout France virtually close down at lunch-time, so don't expect the shops to be open then.

The French dine or sup from about 7.30 p.m. Even though dinner (*le dîner*) is often a lighter affair, it is no less important. As you leave a shop to go home for dinner, the shopkeeper will not only wish you a good evening ('*Bonsoir!*'), but '*Bon appetit!*' as well. And you'd be very unlikely to receive a telephone call from a French person at meal-times. In fact, the telephone is so little used at lunch-time that a cheaper rate operates over the lunch break for calls within France. If you need to phone a French person at home at meal-times, excuse yourself for interrupting: '*Pardonnez-moi de vous avoir dérangé.*'

French people have a long tradition of going out for celebratory feasts *en famille* – sometimes in the evening, but more usually at Sunday lunch-time or on public holidays – and then the cheaper menus, for hungry but exacting workers, may not be available.

WHAT DO THE FRENCH EAT?

What the French actually eat depends to a large extent on the region in which they live. Burgundians are likely to casserole their beef or chicken in a rich sauce based on the red wine of that region, whereas the cooking of Alsace is more likely to reflect the quality of their local white wines. Cooking in the coastal regions of Brittany concentrates on the simple presentation of delicious fresh fish. Much of the cooking of the south-west features duck and goose, often preserved in its own grease (*confit*), while cooks from Lyon tend to favour the pig (*all* of it, including the trotters). In Provence meat is often cooked very simply in the oven, but the juices are put to wonderful use as sauces to accompany the vegetables. And Provençal olive oil is second to none.

Products such as breakfast cereals, which were once hardly eaten at all in France, are becoming increasingly popular, especially among the young, who are rejecting the traditional French breakfast of *croissants*, or bread with jam, and hot, milky coffee (*café au lait*) or chocolate (*chocolat chaud*). The consumption of prepared and convenience foods rises year by year. In spite of all this, the French attitude to food is fundamentally different from ours. The French eat out more than the British do, for one thing, and are far more likely to take their children along too. They demand food of a higher quality. They see eating as a pleasurable activity to be enjoyed for its own sake, rather than as a necessity to be got through with the minimum of fuss.

As a result, French food has more flavour than British food. Free-range maize-fed chicken (*poulet fermier*) has a tougher texture than at home. You might not even recognize it as chicken in a blindfold test. But this is what chicken is actually like, and once you're used to eating it, the moist, bland product served up in Britain may seem little more than a mass-produced imitation. Chicken in France costs about twice as much as it does in England, and this says a lot about the French and their food. Even the fruit and vegetables are different. There is nothing to compare with the flavour of fresh beans (*haricots*) in France, and tomatoes (*tomates*) are wonderfully positive and tangy.

It's usually pointless to generalize about any aspect of a country as large and varied as France. Having said that, French home cooking is based on good quality ingredients simply prepared and presented, inexpensive but carefully chosen wine served in unpretentious glasses, and a respect for and pleasure in the food that will spread into and involve every member of the family.

CAN WE DRINK THE WATER?

Water has been a talking-point for quite some time in France, especially in the south. The problem is that many areas are suffering a drought that is almost unprecedented. Restrictions and bans are wide-ranging, but agriculture in particular is paying a high price.

Water is supplied by private companies, and is as safe to drink as it is in the UK. So why is it that many French people would never dream of drinking water from the tap? Why are some people unwilling even to cook their vegetables in it? And should you follow their example?

There are two main reasons why the French do not drink tap water. The first is simply habit. Amazingly enough, it was only comparatively recently that mains water was made safe to drink. As little as fifteen years ago holiday-makers visiting certain parts of the country were being warned about the quality of the drinking water, and quite rightly so. Now old habits die hard: the French have long been in the habit of drinking bottled mineral water and it would take more than the improved quality of mains water to change that!

Secondly, although the water companies say that the water is safe to drink, a school of thought exists that maintains otherwise. The theory is that, in certain regions, notably where there is a lot of agriculture, the mains water contains high levels of chemicals, especially nitrates. It's said that these come from fertilizers and other chemicals used on the land, and are washed by rain into the water-table. Not surprisingly, the water suppliers maintain one view and opposing lobbies maintain another. And don't forget, exactly the same controversy now rages in Britain. . .

There's little doubt, however, that the mains water is clean in the bacteriological sense, which is to say that drinking it won't give you a stomach upset. And if you choose to believe the nitrates lobby, you could argue that a couple of weeks isn't going to hurt anyway. If not, see below for the various types of bottled waters.

WINES, BEERS AND OTHER INTERESTING BOTTLES

Visitors to France, young and old, come home raving about cheap drink. In fact, cheap wine and beer are not exclusively French attractions. It's more that, so far as alcohol is concerned, Britain is one of Europe's more expensive countries.

NON-ALCOHOLIC DRINKS

Fruit juice (*jus de fruit*) is the same as at home. The most usual types are orange juice (*jus d'orange*), grapefruit (*jus de pamplemousse*), apple juice (*jus de pomme*) and grape juice (*jus de raisin*). You can also get more unusual ones, like apricot (*jus d'abricot*) and blackcurrant (*jus de cassis*). Just ask for '*un jus de . . . s'il vous plaît.*' Drinks that are very refreshing, especially on a hot day, are *orange pressée* and *citron pressé* (freshly squeezed orange or lemon juice) – you add sugar and water yourself – delicious! You may see people sitting outside bars and cafés with a bright green liquid in a glass. This is *menthe à l'eau* (a sort of mint cordial with water) and is also very refreshing. Coca-Cola is *un coca*.

If all you want is a glass of (bottled) water, *eau minérale* is mineral water, *gazeuse* is fizzy, and *plate* or *non-gazeuse* is still. There's not a lot of difference in taste between the still waters, but there is a wide range of flavour among the fizzy waters with some (notably those from Vichy) having a much saltier taste than others. Trial and error is the only way to find your own favourite, but whichever it turns out to be, put it in the fridge as soon as you get home and serve it up nice and cold.

Herb teas (*tisanes* or *infusions*) are drunk throughout the country; the most popular are *verveine* (verbena) and *tilleul* (lime blossom). The French don't drink tea as a rule; if you ask for tea (*un thé*) in a café or restaurant, you might get a cup or glass of hot water with a teabag for you to dunk in it. If you want milk, you'll have to ask for your tea *avec un peu de lait frais* (with a little fresh milk). However, hot chocolate (*chocolat chaud*) and coffee are very good in France, especially with a *croissant* for breakfast. In cafés and restaurants, *un café* means a small cup of espresso coffee, *un café crème*, white coffee, and *un déca* is decaffeinated coffee. If you want hot milk in it, which the French have only as a breakfast drink, ask for *un café au lait*.

WINE (*le vin*)

France is one of the world's great wine producers. The French think of their wine as they do their food: nothing can compare with it. Some countries, it's true, try hard, but. . . A characteristic shrug expresses everything. How can they hope to rival the best?

This attitude brings about some curious results. The most unexpected one is that, leaving aside the question of price, of the two Britain is probably the more interesting country in which to buy wine. This is because it's difficult to buy any wine in France other than French wine. You might see a few of the better known Italian bottles here and there, but they are very rare. So if your taste extends to a nice Rioja, or to the many excellent Bulgarian, Australian or American wines, don't bother looking for them in France.

If you are a knowledgeable wine-lover, you will have brought with you a large number of authoritative British books on French wines (the British connoisseur can beat the French one at this game). You will establish yourself somewhere where world-renowned vineyards cluster – and will spend your days touring and tasting. This section is for people who like a glass or two of decent wine with their food, from time to time, without making a tremendous fuss about it. And as France is the world's greatest wine producer. . .

Strange but true, if you want to pay £15 or more for a bottle of French wine, you can do as well or better in Britain if you buy from a reputable merchant (and some British supermarket chains do a good, careful job, too). The reasons are too technical to go into here, but it's all to do with tax systems. And it's only in very big French towns that you'll find a proper posh wine merchant's shop. The real French connoisseur has his crates sent to him from the *château* or the vineyard, and lays them down in his cellar. He wouldn't think of just popping out to buy a bottle of some great vintage, and anyway he'd find it hard to do so in most parts of France.

It's where you descend to the sort of table wine that costs around £2–3 a bottle in Britain that you score in France. There are plenty of bottles of such good healthy stuff on the supermarket shelves at 10F or less. There, too, you will find wine which can be just as good, put up in plastic 1½-litre (2½-pint) bottles (= two normal wine bottles) at a good deal less per glass. (Bottling, corking, labelling, etc., costs the producer about 4F per normal wine bottle.) And if you're in a wine-producing area where you see wineries inviting you to come in for *une dégustation gratuite*, a free wine-tasting, you might be able to buy it 'loose' (*en vrac*) straight from the pump, at 5F the litre or so. But they won't sell you less than 5 litres (1 gallon) like that, or sometimes 10, and you'd need your own jerrycan – and then you'd need to bottle it somehow, because once you've poured some out of your jerrycan you've let the air in and it won't take more than a couple of days to start turning to vinegar. However, some of these wineries will supply a 10- or 15-litre (2- or 3-gallon) 'bag in box', which lets wine out without letting air in. (See also WINE AND DRINKS in Chapter 7).

WINE REGIONS (*les régions des vins*)

Of all the wine-producing regions of France, most of the finest wines come from the Loire, Bordeaux, Burgundy and the Rhône valley and, of course, from Champagne. But vines are found over most of France and virtually the whole of the southern third of the country produces wine of one sort or another, although much of it, to the connoisseur at least, is of dubious quality. If you are visiting a wine region, a fair amount of space in the supermarket will be devoted to the local wines. In the south-west, for example, leaving aside Bordeaux, there are some excellent red wines from Cahors and dry white ones from Gaillac.

Further east are found the regions of Minervois, Corbières and Fitou. These are among the chief contributors to the European 'wine lake', but can be good, depending on the producer. A huge amount of cheap table wine is produced throughout Languedoc-Roussillon each year and, although much of it is blended with other wines and exported, a fair amount is knocked back at home, too. The red wines are more reliable than the whites, many of which can have an unpleasantly acidic nature, although *rosé* from Minervois can be very pleasant. Other good *rosé* wines are produced further east still, in Provence.

WINE LABELS

On a label, AOC (or AC) means *Appellation d'Origine Contrôlée* (or *Appellation Contrôlée*). And that means that the vine-grower and winemaker have observed the fairly stringent conditions for that particular area. Simple 10F bottles can come in this class, as well as noble bottles costing a pop-star's ransom. The next group down has VDQS on the label, which stands for *Vin Délimité de Qualité Supérieure*, supposedly those wines that are not as good as AOC, but which are better than *vins de pays*.

Vin de pays (country wine) simply means that the wine comes from one particular area, unblended with wine from elsewhere. This is a lower category than AOC or VDQS, in theory; but some *vins de pays* can be better (and dearer) than some AOCs.

Vin de table (table wine) means just *vin ordinaire*, or plonk. It's a misleading name, because the noblest AOCs are table wines too, in the sense that you drink them with meals. Anyway, the wine will be blended. Not that there's anything wrong with that; a weakish wine with a nice flavour and a hint of bouquet needs a good dose of something less distinguished but stronger, or it won't keep. You might easily find a wine in this official classification that pleases you as well as one of the humbler AOCs. These are the wines most usually sold in plastic bottles. On some you may see *vin de plusieurs pays de la CEE* – a blend of wine from several EEC countries. It will at least be drinkable and quite good for stewing tough chunks of beef in.

Wine for drinking with meals is dry (*sec*), and that is how almost all red (*rouge*) and *rosé* wines come. White wines (*vins blancs*) can be dry or – for drinking with dessert or as an *apéritif* – sweet (*doux*) or semi-sweet (*moelleux* or *demi-sec*).

SPARKLING WINES (*vins mousseux*)

Mousseux means sparkling. Champagne is the most famous *vin mousseux*, and costs at least three-quarters of the British price. Champagne comes from a region in the north-eastern quarter of the country, with its centre in the city of Reims. It's probably the most famous wine in the world, associated in most people's minds, the French included, with a celebration of some sort. If you are holidaying in that region it certainly makes sense to buy champagne from the producer (see WINE

AND DRINKS, Chapter 7), but don't expect to get a fantastic bargain. There's no need to discount it to get rid of the stuff, and it's expensive in France, just as it is at home.

Other *vins mousseux*, made by the labour-intensive *méthode champenoise* but not in the Champagne district, can cost only half their British price – around 30F the bottle. These can be good value. Blanquette de Limoux (see below), Clairette de Die and many *vins mousseux*, *méthode champenoise* wines from the Loire (for example, Veuve Amiot or Ackermann from near Saumur, and others from Vouvray) can be served with confidence to people who are not connoisseurs of champagne, and are quite as good as cheap champagnes costing around 60F. Below these there are cheap sparkling wines at around 10F or less, not made by the champagne method. These are, frankly, inferior factory-made products – but they come in champagne bottles with corks that go pop and provide simple fun with the *pâtisserie* course. (Real French fizzy farm cider from Normandy, in similar bottles – *le cidre bouché* – costs as much, and is worth trying if you can find it – see below.)

Blanquette de Limoux is an interesting wine which is increasingly available in Britain, and which will tempt many visitors to the south-west. Limoux is a pretty market town with a beautiful central square, lying between Toulouse and Perpignan. The producers of Blanquette claim that it's the oldest *méthode champenoise* wine in France, older than champagne itself. If you like champagne more than you like the price, you may well find Blanquette a more than adequate substitute. And if you were to try the blindfold test you might not even be able to tell which was which – although maybe you have to try many different bottles before you find something as crisp and dry as real champagne. Maybe. Still, the search is very pleasant indeed, especially at 20F or 30F a bottle. Try it and see.

BEER AND CIDER *(la bière et le cidre)*

For those who prefer beer *(la bière)* to wine, France can be something of a disappointment. The vast majority of French beers are brewed in the Alsace region, and are light, lively lagers, generally fairly low in alcohol. It's completely different in character and taste from the darker, heavier ales and stouts of the British Isles, but as Britain becomes more and more a nation of lager drinkers, it may well be that this style of beer will be the norm at home too in the future. And it must be admitted that it's well suited for drinking at a shady pavement café on a hot afternoon.

Without doubt the best place to buy beer is the supermarket (see BEER, Chapter 7). Small grocers will have a few bottles, but little choice, whereas the larger supermarkets sell ordinary beer at extremely low prices and also usually offer a selection of the few dark beers made in France, plus sometimes some foreign ones. It's possible to buy Guinness, for example. Ordinary French beer comes in tiny little 'multi-pack' bottles or in 1-litre (1¾-pint) bottles sold singly. The larger the bottle the cheaper the beer, especially since there is usually money back on the bottle. Taking the deposit into account, the cheapest beers are about 3F50 per litre.

French cider (*le cidre*) is excellent, and well worth trying if you are a cider-lover. There are a wide variety of ciders available, from fizzy to almost totally flat, from sweet to very dry. *Cidre bouché* is the fizzy version; it's very good, but difficult to find outside Normandy. Normandy is the orchard of France and the greatest cider-producing region, as it is of Calvados (see below).

APERITIFS AND OTHER SPIRITS *(les apèritifs)*

For the French, the *apéritif* is an institution, though if you invite French people for an aperitif you'll be surprised at how many of them refuse a top-up. A popular aperitif is *anisette* or *pastis*, an aniseed flavoured spirit. The French way to drink it is with ice plus water. As you drink you add more water so that the final sips are more water than *pastis*. It's sold under a number of brand names, the most famous of which are probably Pernod and Ricard, and it's all too easy to get into the habit of drinking it.

Other drinks are the same as at home: gin and tonic is *un gin-tonic*, whisky and soda *un whisky-soda*, vodka *un vodka*, and so on. *Kir* is a mixture of white wine and a blackcurrant liqueur *(cassis)*; *kir royale* is the same with champagne (or a sparkling wine). The French also sometimes drink white port *(porto blanc)* as an aperitif, and *pineau* (a blend of cognac and grape juice).

BRANDY AND DISTILLED LIQUEURS *(eau de vie)*

Brandy is wine that has been distilled, and France produces two of the finest brandies in the world: cognac and armagnac. Cognac comes from the town of Cognac in the Charente, and armagnac from the region of the same name in Gascony. To the connoisseur, there is a world of difference between the various producers of cognac and armagnac, and many profitable hours can be spent touring both regions – which are attractive for all sorts of other reasons, too – finding which of the various houses produces the one that pleases you the most.

Of course, you don't need to buy the best to enjoy brandy, as many regions of France produce their own variety, including an excellent one from Corsica. In fact, liqueurs of many different kinds are to be found in France, some of them, like Cointreau and Bénédictine, very widely known and enjoyed. Alsace produces a whole range of spirits distilled from different fruits, and it is in this region that the lover of liqueurs will find the greatest selection.

Relatively unfamiliar to British travellers, perhaps, is Calvados, from Normandy. This is a distillate of cider, frequently compared to cognac, but preferred by many. It's often called the *trou normand*, or 'Norman hole', in that the purpose of drinking it during the meal is said to be to make a nice hole in the heavy Norman fare, which you can then fill with even more food.

EATING OUT

One of the main reasons for choosing to holiday in France is the food. It is, after all, one of the world's great centres – the French would say *the* great centre – of food and cooking. The quality of fresh food to be found in greengrocers, butchers, markets and supermarkets is outstanding, a golden opportunity to prepare excellent food yourself.

Shopping and cooking abroad may be an adventure, but washing-up isn't. Self-caterers like to eat out sometimes. France invented restaurants and cafés, and there are a lot of them around – more per head than in Britain, even now when the Chinese and the Indians have made it possible to eat almost any day at almost any time, almost anywhere. There are a few Arab and Chinese (usually Vietnamese, in fact) restaurants in biggish towns, but if you want to eat 'ethnic' in France, you'll almost certainly be disappointed. The vast majority of restaurants are firmly French.

The French have an attitude to food that is all their own. It is not simply that they seem to enjoy food more than we do, and they certainly don't necessarily eat more. But as individuals they are so very concerned with it. They talk about it a lot. A visit to a new town will be discussed afterwards on the basis of the restaurants and the quality of the fresh food to be had there. Most French people are very knowledgeable about what goes into a particular dish and how it's prepared, and will discuss at length the relative merits of different foods, and where to find them at their best.

When a French person goes to a restaurant, what matters most is the quality of the food, not the surroundings. After the food, the service is almost as important. Good service in a French restaurant is simple and unobtrusive, allowing you to enjoy the food without any distraction. A combination of good food and good service makes for a busy, successful restaurant.

Even for quite experienced diners, taking a dictionary with you is not a bad idea. The fact that the French eat frogs' legs and snails has become quite a joke, but there is nothing to be gained by avoiding the fact that they are happy to eat many things which some of us would find revolting. The restaurant in Paris called Au Pied de Cochon serves, as its name suggests, pigs' trotters prepared in any number of utterly delicious ways, but the very idea of pigs' trotters will not appeal to some. You might well come across a tasty starter called *museau de boeuf*. Many of us would recognize the word '*boeuf*' and assume that anything to do with beef ought to be good, which is true in this case. But *museau* means 'muzzle', which might make some people think again.

This is not to encourage you to be conservative about what you eat. Stay with roast chicken and you might as well stay at home. But tastes do differ, and you need to understand the menu to get the best out of it, not only to avoid disaster. So take your dictionary.

CHOOSING WHERE TO EAT

Why not plan your eating-out in 'proper' restaurants seriously, as a French person would? If you're staying near a medium-sized town, wander around one day at lunch-time, plotting where to go tomorrow. Read menus. See which restaurants are full of happy-looking French people. Note their closing day (*fermeture hebdomadaire le lundi* – weekly closing day Monday). Book a table ('*Je voudrais réserver une table pour quatre, pour demain, à midi et demi*' – 'I'd like to reserve a table for four, for tomorrow at 12.30'). (Use the 24-hour clock for evening bookings.)

Have confidence in the French customer. Restaurants that appear to be doing a roaring trade among the locals are probably good value. If the weather's fine, they may be eating outside; otherwise, peep through the window. Places in prominent locations in touristy spots, especially if they have what appear to be bargain menus in English, German and Dutch, can be a rip-off (the menu won't cost more than it says outside, but the food will show evidence of short cuts via the tin and the deep-freeze).

LE RESTAURANT

In 1990 prices the range runs from 50F to 500F. If you are a 'foodie' who cheerfully stumps up £100 for two in smart restaurants at home, you will have armed yourself with the current year's red *Guide Michelin*, and perhaps *Le Guide Gault Millau*, and you will have prepared your visits to top 500F places. If they're not in either of those bibles, or if you can get a table without booking three weeks ahead, summer or winter, you won't go there. You'll have few language problems, partly because your interest in gourmet food will already have made you only too familiar with restaurant French, and partly because the personnel speak many languages and are used to looking after wealthy foreigners.

It's at the small family-run place, with weekday lunch menus at 100F or less, that with luck you will get the greatest value in pleasure-for-money. The law compels all restaurants to exhibit priced menus outside. Usually there will be two or three menus at different prices, and perhaps a priced list of *à la carte* dishes. (Choosing from the *à la carte* list is more expensive than having one of the menus of the day – see THE MENU, below.) Although there are still a few places, usually in plonk-producing areas, that provide a jug of wine 'free' with the 60 or 70F menu, and many more places that supply wine by the jug (*vin en pichet*) at low prices, you may feel that you are being stung for drinks when you are charged about four times the shop price for wine, beer or bottled mineral water. That should be the only surprise. Well, not really a surprise, because the wine-and-drinks list (which *doesn't* have to be shown outside) does show the price. The restaurateur here may be offering menus that provide excellent value, and he aims to make his main profit on the drinks. If you stick to tap water, which must by law be provided free, you will disappoint him. . .

Some restaurants offer no choice at all. You can find these by asking around among local people, or by looking out for signs saying *table d'hôte* – literally, 'at the host's table'. These signs typically lead to a farmhouse off the beaten track, where you eat in a small dining-room around an open fire. You usually have to book a couple of days beforehand, when you'll be told what the menu will be. Vegetables and fruit will probably be home produced, and this can apply to the meat and butter too. It can feel like the family dining-room (it usually is) and not everyone finds this comfortable, but it's difficult to imagine anything better than a joint of farm-raised lamb cooked with herbs freshly picked from the cook's garden, with a starter, cheese, home-made dessert, coffee and wine, and all for 130F.

Many small towns have restaurants that are mainly aimed at local workers. These can be unprepossessing places, and you might not recognize them as restaurants were it not for the fact that they are packed with people happily eating. There is often no choice of things to eat. You simply go in, find as many empty places as you need and wait for food to be brought to you, probably starting with a large tureen of soup (*soupe* or *potage*) and several bowls. You need hardly speak at all. The main course may be a stew or casserole (*un ragoût*) of beef or chicken, but don't expect the best cut. It will be served with simple vegetables on one plate, or with chips (*pommes frites*). A dessert (*un dessert*), a little simple cheese (*du fromage*), or even both, will follow. A jug or bottle of wine will be placed on the table to which you help yourself. Coffee will be served at the end. A meal like this can cost as little as 30F, and it would be unreasonable to expect the best for that sum. But these are always thriving places, the food is wholesome, simple and tasty, and the value for money is outstanding. They tend to be open only at lunch-time.

LA BRASSERIE

Brasseries are found in biggish towns. While they may provide a standard unchanging menu (perhaps with a 'dish of the day', *un plat du jour*) they mainly go in for grills, fairly elaborate salads (*salades*), and often oysters (*huîtres*). They don't provide such good value for money as the better sort of small family-run restaurant, but you're in and out quicker.

They're convenient, especially for something-with-chips, a glass of beer (*une bière*) and a factory-made ice cream (*une glace*). Always in prominent positions, they can be good spots for watching the world go by.

Le Bar

The border line between low-key brasseries and up-market bars is fairly hazy. Every small town and many villages have a bar, often situated in the main square, and many will serve food. A single dish of the day – *plat du jour* – may be served, or snacks such as *croque monsieur* (a toasted cheese and ham sandwich), or both. You will drink beer or local wine with your meal, and feed a family for the cost of a single meal in a posh restaurant. Many bars serve meals only at lunch-time, but will do snacks throughout the day. And if all you want is a cup of coffee, you will be equally welcome. '*Un café, s'il vous plaît*' will produce a small, black coffee. If you want white, ask for *un café crème*.

If you are eating in a bar, whether you sit inside or at a table in the street, simply take your place and wait for the waiter to come to you. Some bars have areas set aside for food, and if you sit there you will be expected to eat, but there are always tables just for drinks too. If no menu is displayed ask for *le menu, s'il vous plaît*. If there is a *plat du jour* and you can't see what it is, ask *Quel est le plat du jour?* '*Compris*' means 'included', '*non compris*', 'not included'.

The cost of eating in a bar is usually very reasonable. In Paris and other cities it varies according to location, but will in any case be more expensive than in a small country town or village, as it also will in a region that's very touristy. Eating the *plat du jour*, with a dessert, coffee and drinking beer or local wine is likely to cost between 30F and 60F per head, with most bars in the lower price bracket in rural areas. For dedicated bargain-hunters with the right 'nose' it is still possible to find a simple dish of the day such as local sausage (*saucisse*) and mashed potatoes (*pommes mousseline*) with coffee for as little as 20F.

CAFETERIAS *(les cafeterias)*

Cafeterias on motorways are best avoided. With a few honourable exceptions they offer inferior food at inflated prices. But some cafeterias attached to hypermarkets and big supermarkets – Casino, especially – can be surprisingly good (and well patronized by French locals, so there may be long queues at proper French meal-times but with lots of room at 1.30 p.m.). You will probably find iced water on tap, little microwave ovens so that you can warm up your second course if it's got cold, and high chairs for toddlers. And of course there's no language problem: you see the food and help yourself, or just point if assistants are serving it. There's wine (over-priced, as usual, in bottle, but also available cheap from the serve-yourself tap, in ¼-litre jugs), beer and Coca-Cola, and the usual range of soft drinks.

LE FAST-FOOD

Yes, *le fast-food* has arrived. Branches of McDonalds, and imitations, can be seen in big towns, and pizzerias have sprung up everywhere. Some young French people think it *très chic* to scandalize their elders by consuming hamburgers and milk shakes at improper meal-times. Well, you know all about those. They are a bit dearer than in Britain.

THE MENU *(le menu)*

The menu is *le menu*. To ask for it, say '*le menu, s'il vous plaît*'. Most restaurants offer a choice of set meals. A typical menu will have a set meal at 55F, one at 85F and one at 115F (or thereabouts). Naturally the ingredients will be more exotic in the higher price brackets. So if you want to try *foie gras*, don't look for it on the 55F menu. The menu will state clearly that service is included *(service compris)*. A ¼-litre (½-pint) jug of house wine is sometimes included too (it will say *vin compris*), usually with the cheaper meals.

The rest of the menu lists individual dishes from which you can choose if the set meals do not appeal. Eating a set meal is usually substantially cheaper than eating *à la carte*, which you can see by comparing the prices. There is no difference in the size of the portion.

When the waiter comes to take your order, make it clear from which part of the menu you are ordering. For example, say '*trois menus à quatre-vingt cinq francs, s'il vous plaît*' ('three 85F menus, please') before the rest of the party orders in the normal way. When ordering, it's quite all right to point to items on the menu, if you can't pronounce the name.

SERVICE

Many small hotels and restaurants in France are run as family businesses, so it's quite possible that the person who takes your order is the proprietor, and her husband/his wife is in the kitchen preparing the food. These people don't expect to get rich, but to make a reasonable living in a proud and noble profession. Food is respected by the French, and those who buy, prepare, cook and serve it are important people. There is nothing menial about being a waiter. He is at your service, and will see to your wants to the best of his ability, but he is neither your servant nor your master, neither obsequious nor overbearing.

All the same, the French have strong views about what is proper as regards food, and particularly as regards wine. Some people have encountered waiters who refuse to serve a particular wine with a particular food. This is rare, but sufficiently embarrassing as to spoil a meal for most of us. If you choose the house wine (*vin de table*) it simply won't happen, and anyone who knows enough to make a reasoned choice from a wine list isn't likely to have a problem either. It is only a bad choice of a fine, expensive wine that is likely to upset a waiter. If you know what you are ordering you should go ahead, but if not, it makes sense to ask your waiter's advice anyway ('*Qu'est-ce que vous nous conseillez comme vin?*'). And why not do this with the cheaper wines, too? Look at the list first and give him a price band to work in (*un vin dans les environs de quarante francs* – a wine in the region of 40F), and don't feel humiliated because you don't want to pay very much. Your value as a customer is never calculated according to how much money you spend.

French service at its best is attentive but discreet. You will be brought everything you really need. You will not be asked to taste a house wine. The waiter may not even pour it for you, and he is most unlikely to refill your glass later. Besides, do you really want him hovering over you ready to leap forward and light your cigarette? He doesn't do these things because he is too busy serving food. French restaurants are not over-staffed and the waiter is on the go the whole time, serving food, wine, coffee and water almost at a run. Your waiter forgetting something should prompt a gentle reminder rather than an outraged demand.

Unless things are exceptionally busy and the person in charge seems rushed off her or his feet, don't be afraid to discuss at some length what you want to eat. In a proper restaurant, even a cheap one, they want you to be happy.

ETIQUETTE

At any proper restaurant, however cheap, hang around after you've entered and wait to be shown to a table. Apparently empty ones may have been reserved; and anyway this is when the person in charge of the dining-room makes your acquaintance.

The French have always eaten out regularly, unlike the British, many of whom still go to restaurants only on special occasions. They do not dress up to eat out, and provided you are clean and reasonably tidy no-one will take the slightest notice of how you are dressed. Only in elegant restaurants need gentlemen bother with a jacket and tie – and even then, after they've had a look around, they may feel happy to dispense with one or both. On the other hand, it's only in seaside cafés that bare-chested gentlemen in jeans torn off above the knee will be tolerated (and even then will be looked on as barbarians; ears will be bent to discover what horrible region they come from). Otherwise, don't worry; on holiday the French dress informally.

Don't call the waiter *garçon*! He is *Monsieur*. The waitress is *Mademoiselle*, unless you think she would be happier to be called *Madame* (as a probably married lady).

ON THE TABLE

In restaurants, bread is on the table (free) in chunks, renewed as required. And salt and pepper. Absolutely no British-type bottled sauces – they wouldn't suit the food and would kill the wine, being based on vinegar and sugar. (Alkalines, such as cheese, make wine taste better; acids make it taste horrid and so do sugars, unless it's a sweet wine. But hamburger joints have tomato ketchup, and most cafeterias have a help-yourself table of vinaigrettes and so on to go with salad.) Mustard may be there, or you may have to ask for it (*de la moutarde, s'il vous plaît*).

In simple restaurants the table-cloth might be paper (renewed for each customer) and you might find that you have to use the same knife and fork for more than one course (though not after fish). Such economies are disappearing, but they are not necessarily a bad sign – the serious and economical French eater wants time and trouble devoted to the cooking, not to the frills.

Any water brought to the table will be from the tap. If you want mineral water you should order it with your food – *eau minérale, gazeuse, non-gazeuse* (mineral water, fizzy, still). There will be no side plates, as bread is simply broken and laid on the cloth. There will be no butter either, though some might be brought later with the cheese. If you want butter (*du beurre, s'il vous plaît*), the waiter will bring it (as he will bring whatever you ask for, within reason), but you will have to excuse him if he thinks you a little strange. Unless you request otherwise, coffee (*un café*) will be served strong and black in a tiny cup, and asking for white coffee (*un café crème*) can increase the cost of a cheap meal by a quite remarkable percentage.

THE BILL *(l'addition)*

At the end of the meal ask the waiter for the bill *(l'addition, s'il vous plaît)* and pay him, although if the place is busy you might have to wait for him to come back to you. If you are in a hurry it's quite in order to go to the counter and pay.

Do check the bill. Mistakes occur, especially in simple, busy places. Usually these are genuine mistakes, and quite often in your favour (in which case you will make friends and influence people if you point out the mistake). Rectification and apologies will normally ensue. But it could be your mistake, usually with items from the wine list (one Briton we once observed had thought that *vin compris* – wine included – meant that he could drink the most expensive bottle from the list, free, instead of his ration of plonk).

Service *(service)* is always included, unless you see '*service non compris*' on the menu, so there's no tip required nor expected, unless you've demanded and got something out of the run in the way of service. Optionally, a few small coins from the change can be left. But do please say '*au revoir!*' – unless, of course, you've made the mistake of going to a rip-off joint that aims at making a quick killing in the tourist season. Such places do exist – but they're not difficult to spot from the outside, and if there's a 'barker' in front using fractured English to lure you in, flee to where the French eat.

CHAPTER SEVEN

GOING SHOPPING FOR FOOD

There's a lot of food and drink in France. Up in the frozen north, with a climate like Birmingham, there are cows and sugar beet; down in the south, grapes and olives. At the edges (the Atlantic, the Channel, the Mediterranean) there are soles, oysters and tuna fish. In the middle there are all kinds of things, from wheat and sheep to truffles and stout-legged frogs (the latter are an occasional luxury as starters). Cheese springs up everywhere that cows, sheep or goats can be led to a milking machine. France has almost everything one needs on its home ground, except coffee, tea and whisky (well, there *is* French whisky, but everybody drinks the Scotch variety, and the local imitation is not on sale in most shops), so abandon any notion that you'll have to go without something.

There are supermarkets in every small town, with all these French things plus a variety of fresh, canned and deep-frozen things from favoured parts of the food-exporting world. Villages, small towns and big towns have markets. Bakers bake fresh bread every day. The French eat more meat than the British, and they also eat more fresh fruit and vegetables (but fewer potatoes). The self-caterer will not starve, even on an exclusive diet of fish fingers, Heinz tomato sauce and Coca-Cola. And if you and your family take food and drink seriously, you are in perhaps the best place to do so. This chapter should give you plenty of help.

OPENING HOURS

It helps all round in France if you take the French timetable into consideration – especially when shopping. To generalize boldly: the French start work at 8 a.m. and press on without a break until 12. Then they have a proper meal, usually the main meal of the day. Back to work at 2 p.m. for an unbroken stretch until 6. In the country, farm people who are their own bosses make an earlier start, especially in summer and in the south, and take a longer midday break, perhaps with a siesta.

If you're intending to take a shopping trip, you should leave home early enough to have your shopping finished by midday. You can then join the shopkeepers in their leisurely lunch, perhaps sitting in some shady pavement café. Alternatively, you can have lunch at home and aim to arrive in town by about 3 p.m. Most of the traders will be back at their posts by then, and you can wander round the shops until 7.30 or so without much problem.

Your little village shop is there to do business by serving its faithful customers. It may open at 7.30 a.m. and close for lunch at 12.15 or 12.30, so that people who have to go to work can pop in, before or after. It will then close, with a sigh of hungry relief . . . and it might not open again until 3 or even 4 p.m., closing again around 7 or 8 in the evening. It will almost certainly open on Sunday morning – and be closed on Monday morning, or all day Monday, in exchange. (Sunday lunch is the finest meal of the week, so people just *have* to be able to shop; but they ought to be able to have enough over to avoid starvation on Mondays.)

Small specialist shops, run by the boss with her or his family and an apprentice, may do much the same, even in quite big towns. The baker is again a prime example. So, indeed, are the smaller supermarkets, especially those in a small town, whose principal customers are people who live within a couple of minutes' walk.

Right at the other extreme is the mighty hypermarket,

whose customers all come by car and load their trollies with a week's provisions. This will probably be open all day from 9 a.m. until 7 p.m., or as late as 10 p.m. on one or two days a week (probably Friday and/or Saturday). It will be closed all day Sunday, but open on Monday (when its most noticeable clients will be bright pink or deep red foreigners from the campsite, baffled by the normal French timetable at the other shops).

PRICES

What will you spend on foodstuffs, compared with what you normally spend at home? An impossible question. There's the rate of exchange, for one thing. If the pound falls and the franc rises, everything becomes dear in France for the visiting Briton, but cheap in Britain for the French. At least, for a while. Vice versa, and France is full of bargains (temporarily).

In both countries, imported things can cost more than in the country where they were produced. Let Madame A go to England while Mrs B goes to France; let them fill their shopping baskets with as nearly as possible the same things as they would have done at home and each will exclaim 'How dear it is here!'. But that difference is being ironed out, because Britain and France are both members of the EEC; taxation on goods is slowly being harmonized and customs barriers abolished. Ten years ago in France, Scotch whisky was dearer than French cognac. Now it is cheaper, because whisky is cheaper to produce, and EEC directives forbid France to discriminate, tax-wise, against spirits produced in Britain. (Both, by the way, are somewhat cheaper than in Britain.) EEC legislation doesn't mind that ordinary French wine costs vastly more in Britain than in France, so long as we tax the product of Kentish vineyards just as heavily.

At the time of writing (late 1990), lamb and mutton are dearer in France than in the UK. Sheep thrive better in our green and drizzly land. French sheep-farmers are fighting a bitter battle to prevent too many British imports. (For how long will their demonstrations succeed?)

Still, if you take it that fruit and vegetables are cheaper (and often better) in France, while meat and factory-made foodstuffs a bit dearer, you won't be far wrong. France is a wonderful country for the stuff grown in market gardens, which Britain has to import – and transport and distribution costs are relatively high with bulky perishables.

In France, go to the market and buy what's in season and locally produced. On 8 August 1990, Sainsbury's in Britain proudly advertised 'beef' tomatoes at *only* 55p per 1lb. On that day, at the market in a town of 6000 inhabitants near Montpellier, excellent local open-air tomatoes were selling at 4F per 1kg (nearly 2lb). The bank was giving 9.50F for £1, so that's under 17½p per 1lb. 'Best buys', as reported in a British paper of that week, were substantially undercut in the market, if they were fruit and veg. in season. However, Marks & Spencer in the UK were praised for 'fine asparagus' at £1.99 for 6oz. There was no asparagus in the market, but in May it had been about £1.99 for 1kg – which is 35oz. (May is when the local crop is picked.) There were no USA black plums, which Britain's Asda was selling at 99p the lb, but you could get local greengages slightly cheaper, local strawberries and raspberries at £1 for 1lb, and redcurrants at £1.50.

The seasons are about the same as in southern England, and up to three weeks earlier near the Mediterranean. In season, France can produce most of the fruit and vegetables it needs. It's not yet as enterprising as Britain when it comes to imports from across the globe, but things are changing. Twenty years ago, villagers in the south wouldn't have dreamed of asking for tomatoes before July, when the local open-air ones get ripe; indeed, they thought imported greenhouse ones were immoral and probably bad for you. Now they buy them all the year round, paying the price.

Finding really high quality expensive foodstuffs is easier in France. We are more puritanical in these matters; they are more self-indulgent. But there can be quite a wide price-range for the same quality item in France. The canny French person spends time and trouble in economical preparation for self-indulgence, and shops around. Of course, you won't expect the convenient little village shop to be as cheap as the big supermarket for packaged goods, but it pays to compare while strolling in the high street and the market.

TYPES OF SHOP

SUPERMARKETS *(supermarchés)*

The term 'supermarket' covers everything from what was once an old-fashioned general shop in a little village, now reorganized on superkmarket lines (most items pre-packed; you help yourself, putting the items in one of the baskets provided, and present yourself at *la caisse*, the check-out) to mighty *hypermarchés* (hypermarkets) where you can get anything from a packet of salt to a three-piece suite.

The biggest supermarkets are usually to be found in characterless modern commercial zones a mile or two outside big and medium-sized towns. Carrefour, Géant Casino, Mammouth, Auchan and Intermarché are some of the chains. But quite big supermarkets (*supermarchés*) with big car parks, trolleys (*chariots*) freed by putting a 10F coin in the slot (you get it back when you put the trolley back) and computerized check-outs that give you an itemized and priced list of what you've bought, occur on the outskirts of quite small towns (4000 inhabitants upwards, depending on the region). In addition to pre-packed fresh meat, poultry, *charcuterie* (ham, bacon, sausages, *pâtés* and other delicatessen items) and cheese, there are counters for people who prefer to have such things cut and weighed for them.

When choosing fruit and vegetables, help yourself to the things you want and put them in plastic bags. The usual procedure is that you then put each bag on a weighing machine close by, and press the appropriate button for the item – there's usually a little picture by the button, but anyway you can check what it's called, because a notice above the pile of apples or whatever will give you the name and the price per kg; if the price is *la pièce*, i.e. per item, you won't need to weigh it. The machine will print a label for you to stick on the bag. Pay at the check-out.

Such places don't offer much in the way of human warmth or conversation about politics and the weather, but they're convenient, especially for people who know little or no French. You can see everything. Tins have pictures on them. So do ready-cooked deep-frozen dishes – though you need to look at the instructions on the back of the packet. If you want 'boil-in-a-bag', the packet will say that the food can be heated *au bain-marie*, which literally is 'in a double saucepan', but in fact means 'at simmering temperature'. If it says something like *chauffez votre four à 200°C* it's telling you to heat your oven, and *enlevez le couvercle* is remove the lid. References to *un four à micro-ondes* are about how to deal with the food in a microwave oven, but it's unlikely that you'll have one of those in your *gîte*.

A few main items might be on sale in packages with no picture, just words. These are:

flour	*la farine*
milk (UHT, in cardboard cartons)	*le lait*
ready-ground coffee	*le café moulu*
roasted coffee beans	*le café en grains*
sugar	*le sucre*

MARKETS *(marchés)*

Markets provide some of the special pleasures of the self-catering life in France. In small towns there will be a weekly or twice-weekly market, in the market square or in streets temporarily out-of-bounds to motor traffic. Fruit and vegetables are the main things, with meat, poultry and fish from travelling merchants or direct from the producer (or the fisherman's wife, near a port). In the summer, where there are tourists, salesmen will try to charm you into buying dubious plastic souvenirs made somewhere in the Far East. All the year round there are household articles, durable working clothes, 'bargain' pop cassettes, and lots more.

In bigger towns there will be a permanent market hall, open daily, with permanent stall holders. This is less fun than the small town market, but both kinds are ideal for carefully comparing quality and price, especially of popular items of fruit and vegetables. Unlike in the chain supermarket, you may find the genuinely morning-gathered production of local smallholders.

As with the supermarket, there are almost no language problems. What is on sale is on view, clearly (well, fairly clearly) labelled and priced. For fruit and vegetables, you help yourself (except for fragile items, carefully placed out of your reach) putting them in one of the stall holder's baskets or basins. If you can't understand how much money the stall holder wants from you, he or she will make out a little bill, with 1 looking like 7, and 7 therefore crossed.

SPECIALIST SHOPS

One would have thought that the colossal development of supermarkets, and especially of hypermarkets (more noticeable than in Britain) would have spelt the end of most of France's small shops. It is true that many little groceries have closed, often to be replaced by shops selling electronic goods. But other specialist shops carry on vigorously, providing – and usually making – goods that the French want to buy from an individual bent on satisfying other individuals.

THE TAKEAWAY *(le traiteur, la rôtisserie)*

In medium-sized towns you will find *un traiteur*. He specializes in serving wedding feasts in village halls or delivering dinners for a dozen to your home. He also sells ready-made dishes over the counter, and no French person would be ashamed of occasionally taking advantage of his specialist skills. We can give no particular guidance; no two

115

regions are the same nor are any two *traiteurs*. Just look in the window and see if you are tempted. If your French is up to it, ask for descriptions of mysterious specimens.

Almost all *charcuteries*, and very many butchers' shops, have take-away dishes too. Perhaps there is a Chinese take-away somewhere in Paris, but everywhere else they're French.

FOODS

BREAD *(le pain)*

A shop where bread is sold but not made isn't a *boulangerie*, it's a *dépôt de pain*. Don't buy bread from a *dépôt de pain* (and that includes the supermarket) if you can get to a *boulangerie* (baker). Every respectable village has one (the baker will make deliveries daily to outlying *dépôts* and isolated hamlets) and every small town has several. Once or twice a day a delicious smell drifts out from *la boulangerie*, together with people breaking off little samples from the warm loaves they're taking home. Shop around, experimenting, because no two *boulangers* bake alike, and all have their own specialities.

Names for white loaves are many and various, but the most usual long loaf is *une baguette*. A very thin loaf, almost all crust (splendid at breakfast when it's not more than a couple of hours old) is *une ficelle*. But all the bread is visible in the shop. Point to what you like the look of and say '*Un pain comme ça, s'il vous plaît*' ('A loaf like that, please'). Many bakers make special breads, such as *pain complet* (wholemeal) and *pain de seigle* (rye). They also make *croissants* and the simpler cakes, buns and pastries.

French bread has a thick crisp crust, and inside it's full of holes. It takes the place of the British boiled potato as an accompaniment to main dishes (don't hesitate to mop up the gravy with it!). It's totally unsuitable for making thin bread and butter, or British-style buttered toast. If you must have that, you will have to seek out wrapped, sliced bread (*pain de mie*) in a really big supermarket. It will be sweetish and expensive. Once in a blue moon the French buy some (for making toasted sandwiches). It comes from a distant factory, so do look for the 'sell by' date (*date limite de vente*).

Bakers usually take one day off per week, so in a one-baker village there will be – horror! – one day with no fresh bread. But where there are several bakers, some will close on Monday (the usual day) and others on Sunday, so civilized life can continue throughout the week.

MEAT AND POULTRY *(la viande et la volaille)*

Beef, veal, mutton, lamb, poultry and game are the business of *la boucherie*. Pork and 'delicatessen' are the business of *la charcuterie*. The two shops are sometimes combined. Supermarkets sell the lot, pre-packed and/or with a counter for individual service. At the average price/quality level you can do as well at the supermarket as at the 'proper' shop. But if a small town is big enough to support half a dozen *boucheries* and *charcuteries*, one or two are likely to offer top quality goods at a higher price. In August 1990 we could buy tender but rather tasteless fillet steak at 98F the kg; from noble beasts in the Limousin or the Charolais regions (as good as Aberdeen Angus?) it cost 160F, or nearly £8 for 1lb.

BEEF *(le boeuf)*

It's mainly with beef that you may not recognize what you see. Plain blunt Mr Butcher produces quite different 'joints' from those of elegant Monsieur Boucher. What you get in France is cut along the muscles, not across: no waste, no ration of bone, fat and gristle. What they call *rosbif* (roast beef) is a long cylinder about 10cm (4in) in diameter, neatly bound with string and larded with hard pork fat; it's highly suitable for spit roasting or spit grilling, and easy to carve – you just slice it across.

Bifteck (beefsteak) comes from many odd parts of the animal, some available only because of the French method of surgical dissection to produce joints, and carrying a variety of special names. Price can be your guide, for tenderness if not for flavour. You get no advice from a supermarket shelf, but the 'real' butcher is generous with it.

pour faire griller	for grilling
pour faire à la poêle	for gentle frying
pour faire rôtir	for roasting
pour faire mijoter	for slow stewing

LAMB (*l'agneau*), MUTTON (*le mouton*), VEAL (*le veau*) AND PORK (*le porc*)

Cuts of lamb (*agneau*) and mutton (*mouton*) are easily recognizable. So are veal (*veau*) and pork (*porc*) except when – like *rosbif* – long cuts are prepared for roasting (*pour faire rôtir*).

POULTRY (*la volaille*)

As for poultry, the deep-frozen battery bird seems to have been sneered out of existence. An ordinary fresh battery chicken is *un poulet*, a free-range one is *un poulet fermier*. A boiling fowl is *une poule*. The guinea-fowl (*pintade*) is popular; it looks like a chicken but is rather smaller and dearer. Battery turkey (*dinde*) mainly turns up in pieces. Rabbit (*lapin*) is thought 'nobler' than chicken. All these are easily bought in the supermarket, usually marked *prêt-à-cuire*, 'oven ready'. Otherwise, *effilé* means that the gut has been removed but head, neck, feet and all the giblets are still in place.

OFFAL

The British know about liver (*foie*) and kidneys (*rognons*). Other items of offal cost more in France than at home (and are sold in a neater condition), because the French know that time and care can make them delicious. You will see tripe (*tripes*), brains (*cervelle*), pigs' trotters (*pieds de porc*) and other oddments (perhaps even testicles, politely called *rognons blancs* or 'white kidneys', which British butchers tend to keep for themselves).

HORSEMEAT

You will not be palmed off with horse as a substitute for beef. It is sold at a special horse butcher, *la boucherie chevaline*, or at a special section in the bigger supermarkets, clearly marked *cheval*. It isn't particularly cheap; a few people esteem it highly.

DELICATESSEN MEATS *(la charcuterie)*

La charcuterie is the shop as well as the stuff that's sold there – and usually made there, by *le charcutier* himself. Ham *(jambon)*, sausages for cooking *(saucisse)*, and salami-type sausage for eating as it is *(saucisson)*, various cold cooked meats, a wide variety of take-away dishes (some for eating as they are, some for re-heating), *boudins*, which in the best cases it would be libellous to translate as black puddings, *andouillettes*, which are sausages made of tripe (expensive, some of them) adored by many gourmets, and luxury items such as *foie gras* and caviar. . . One could write a book. Jane Grigson did, in fact: *Charcuterie and French Pork Cookery* (Penguin); it's very stimulating, though in a couple of hundred pages she touches only the fringes of the subject. Different regions have different sorts, so do different *charcuteries* in the same town. Be bold! And don't be afraid to ask for one slice *(une tranche)* of this and that, or just a bit *(un petit peu)*, to taste. If it's a good shop they'll be glad to see you taking a serious interest.

Or of course you can get plastic-packed *charcuterie* items in the supermarket, made in a distant factory. In that case, you're not vastly better off than in England. The supermarket has deep-frozen hamburger 'steaks' too, and factory frank-furters. Not to mention corned beef (called *corned-beef*) in tins of familiar shape – and even spam (Tulip brand, from Denmark).

FISH *(le poisson)*

Most markets have fish stalls, often a picturesque sight. In town you might find a fishmonger's *(une poissonerie)*. Frozen fish is in the supermarket, including fish fingers (*bâtonnets de poisson*). On the whole there's no language problem: the fish are there, under your eyes. Unfamiliar specimens down by the Mediterranean may be for fish soup or *bouillabaisse*, which is restaurant food really, and not to be attempted by the inexperienced on holiday. See MENUS AND RECIPES, Chapter 8, for oysters, trout, tuna and mussels.

Veuillez le vider, s'il vous plaît?	Would you gut it, please?

SHELLFISH *(les coquillages)*

Except perhaps for prawns, lobsters and boiled whelks with 'non-brewed condiment', the British are timid about shellfish. Not so the French. Shellfish of many kinds (*coquillages*) are devoured in restaurants as *un plateau de fruits de mer*. Quite expensive, a big multi-coloured platter with a bottle of cool white wine and rye bread with butter provides an agreeable hour of fiddly feeding. It's usually better on the Atlantic coast than on the Mediterranean. It's hardly to be undertaken by self-caterers, unless they're experienced and have time on their hands.

FRUIT AND VEGETABLES *(fruits et légumes)*

Fresh fruit and vegetables should ideally be bought at a market, where you can stroll around and compare. Failing that, there are specialist shops – though not as many as in earlier days, because supermarkets go in for these items in a big way. (See remarks about buying fruit and vegetables earlier in this chapter.)

Per head, the French consume more fresh fruit and vegetables than the British. They don't seem to have taken so readily to deep-frozen ones, and such as you see are more likely to be in big 1kg (2lb) bags, for taking home to one's own deep-freeze. But there is a good range of canned vegetables (with pictures on the can, making life easy if you don't know the words). French canned peas are rather

different from British ones, and some people grow fond of them. But they are much better if tarted up a bit in the French way: soften a tablespoonful of chopped onion with some small bits of streaky bacon in a little butter or oil, then put the drained peas in to heat through.

Runner beans, like swedes and giant marrows, are absent. 'French beans' are *haricots verts* (literally green beans). You can find *haricots à la sauce tomate*, which are baked beans, but they're slightly different (less sugar, for one thing).

DAIRY PRODUCTS

MILK *(le lait)*

There is no milk round. All by itself as a drink, it is consumed only by small children and foreigners. Normal French people use it in the morning as an ingredient in *café au lait*, and that's that.

There are three kinds: sterilized (*sterilisé*), fresh (*frais* or *pasteurisé*) and untreated (*lait cru*). *Sterilisé* is long-life and is sold in 1-litre (1¾-pint) bottles or cartons. Fresh milk can be got here and there in Normandy and other places, but is difficult to find in some areas. Look in the chiller section, or ask for for *lait frais* or *lait pasteurisé*. *Entier* means full cream, *écrémé* means skimmed and *demi-écrémé* means semi-skimmed. The third kind of milk, *lait cru*, is available more in rural areas than anywhere else. It's untreated (i.e. unpasteurized) and therefore can be thought dangerous.

The usual purchase is UHT semi-skimmed milk in 1-litre cardboard cartons from the supermarket. This is all right in tea and coffee, but isn't up to fresh full-cream Jersey as a nourishing tipple. One can console oneself with the fact that there's quite enough nourishment in the normal French diet, and wallow in Volvic, Badoit and other mineral waters as thirst-quenchers.

CREAM *(la crème)*

Cream, on the other hand, is essential. Again, it is bought at the supermarket. *Crème fraîche* is matured, and thickened by natural fermentation. It's irreplaceable for cooking (see Chapter 8, MENUS AND RECIPES). British-type sterilized cream *(crème liquide, stérilisée)* is much less often used, but you'll find it at the supermarket. It's the stuff to use for whipping – and, if you wish, in tea or coffee, where *crème fraîche* would be quite unsuitable.

CHEESE *(le fromage)*

If you are a cheese-lover you will be happy. The French eat a lot of it, in great variety. In big towns you may find a specialist shop, a *fromagerie*, where you might even find that rarity, a Camembert made of unpasteurized milk *(lait cru)*, expensive but very Camemberty. Otherwise, most supermarkets take a pride in their counter for unpackaged sold-by-weight cheese. They also have a packaged cheese section. There are familiar cheeses (Cantal is rather like Cheddar) but do experiment. If you like Stilton, try Roquefort (at half the price it costs in Britain) with a glass of *sweet* wine – Muscat de Frontignan, for example.

YOGHURT *(le yaourt)*

This is very popular, plain or with chunks of fruit in it. Find it near the cream and butter in the supermarket. It's a factory product, so there's no point in seeking a specialist shop. The French export it to Britain, so you'll probably find familiar brands such as Chambourcy.

BUTTER *(le beurre)*

In dairy regions like Normandy you may be able to taste samples of farm butter, sold 'loose' from giant mounds. Otherwise it's in the supermarket in familiar packets. The best is made from matured cream and has a faintly nutty taste, otherwise it's like the British product. Unsalted butter *(beurre doux)* is more popular than salted *(beurre demi-sel)*.

TEA AND COFFEE *(le thé et le café)*

Weak tea can be found in little expensive packets. It's not really a French drink (except for the dying, if they can't afford champagne). If you can't exist without your morning or afternoon cuppa, then take your tea with you.

The boot is on the other foot, for coffee. If you must, you can get instant coffee *(café soluble)* in the supermarket. But just next to it is real coffee, cheaper than in Britain, and if your self-catering accommodation is a *gîte de France*, or is equipped for French people anyway, you have proper coffee-making equipment there – perhaps including a coffee-grinder. *Café en grains* is unground, *café moulu* is ground. If the variety of coffee-bean is *arabica* (giving a lighter, more aromatic brew) the label will proudly proclaim the fact. Otherwise it'll be *robusta*, a stronger, earthier variety, or a mixture.

CAKES AND PASTRIES *(la pâtisserie)*

Like the *confiserie*, this is where you go for 'home made' luxury. It does a roaring trade. The skilled *pâtissier* is a prosperous and happy man. Real freshly-made fruit tarts, big or small, *éclairs* and a host of other oddments – these aren't terribly expensive, and the French serve them as the 'pudding' course. If they haven't got much money, they treat themselves only at Sunday lunch, which is why you will see queues at the *pâtisserie* around 11 a.m. (after church, for church-goers) on Sunday.

Self-caterer, splurge! No language problem: the price is on the card at the back of the tray, and you only need to point and smile. Today's purchase will not be so nice tomorrow.

But cake, of the long-keeping variety, no. You might find that on the supermarket shelves. There you will also see factories' attempts at making something like *pâtisserie* with a long shelf life. Not bad – Mr Kipling has been seen – but an entirely different proposition. Much cheaper, of course, because factory ingredients cost less than fresh fruit, cream, eggs and liqueurs; but for these sorts of cakes and pastries you're better off in Britain.

CONFECTIONERY *(la confiserie)*

If you trek regularly to Bond Street to stock up on hand-made chocolates with luxury fillings, you will be happy in any medium-sized French town. There you will find a *confiserie* (sweet shop) where they will be delighted to make you up a little selection of their chocolates, presenting it in a nice box tied up with gold string.

Such items are for adults to give to one another on special occasions. They are far too good (well, too expensive) to feed to children. French children get adequately fed twice a day (plus breakfast, and a little *goûter* or snack around 5 to keep them going till 8 p.m. dinner) and have not yet organized themselves to insist on 2–4oz of confectionery per day.

The supermarket has factory-made confectionery. The range is not as wide as in Britain, but there are bars, boxes and bags, some of them internationally familiar (Mars bars, for instance, Quality Street and After Eights).

WINE AND DRINKS

WINE *(le vin)*

If you want to, you can drink very cheaply indeed in France. On the whole, though, you will only notice a significant price difference if you are buying wines that are cheap to start with. What would be cheap French plonk in the UK is absurdly cheap in France itself.

Just about the cheapest wine comes in 5-litre (9-pint) plastic containers, rather like the kind of thing you might keep in the boot of the car in case you run out of petrol. These can cost 25F or even less, and the wine inside them is usually perfectly drinkable. It's this kind of product – *vin de pays* (country wine) and *vin de table* (table wine) – that the French themselves drink in the greatest quantities. This, plus wines one or two rungs up the ladder of quality and price, forms the bulk of French wine production and domestic consumption. So, whatever you might have thought about the French and their wine, it's interesting to reflect that what they drink more than anything else is plonk.

WINE FROM THE SUPERMARKET

Here you will find rather more red wine (*vin rouge*) to choose from than white (*vin blanc*) and considerably more red than white in the cheaper categories. There should be a fairly wide selection of *rosé* (*vin rosé*).

All the finer wines are as expensive in France as they are at home. Your supermarket will have a section devoted to them, which you'll be able to pick out by price and by the fact that the bottles are stored in the proper way, on their sides, with just one bottle upright on display. There are as many differences of opinion about wine as there are producers, and I've no intention of causing a storm of controversy by recommending some here and leaving out others. You will have to discover which wines you like, either by trial and error, or by buying a book on the subject.

BUYING FROM THE PRODUCER

If you are buying a wine for the first time, naturally you will want to try it first. This is impossible in the supermarket, of course, and you need to go either to a wine merchant or to the producer.

It's perhaps not surprising that the yellow pages of the telephone directory (*annuaire*) in a wine-producing region are stuffed with entries of all sorts associated with wine. For a wine merchant you should look under *Vins et spiritueux (vente au détail)* – Wines and spirits (retail sales) – and for the producers *Vins (production et vente directe)* – Wines (production and direct sale). The wine merchant won't look much different from an English one, except that there may well be huge vats lining the walls from which you can fill your *bonbonne* or any other suitable container with wine at the very cheapest prices.

Going to the producer is always fun. Don't expect signs up to tell you what to do. In the main wine-producing areas

(Languedoc, the Loire valley, etc.), many wineries making inexpensive wines exhibit at the roadside big notices: '*Dégustation gratuite*', which means 'free wine tasting'. In the bigger ones there will be an English-speaking hostess. If there's no one in sight when you walk in, you may have to shout – '*Il y a quelqu'un?*' ('Is anyone there?'). When someone appears, say '*Je voudrais déguster des vins, s'il vous plaît*' ('I'd like to taste some wines please'). You will then be given some information about what's available, and the prices, and the rest is up to you. You won't be rushed and, in theory at least, if you don't like anything it won't be held against you.

Do go in and try a sample or two. Buy a bottle if you want to, but don't feel you have to; this is a public relations exercise. They hope you will remember the name of the winery when you are back home, and pounce on it with joy when you see it on British supermarket shelves.

The wine may be no cheaper than it would have been in a large supermarket, but if you feel like it, go to a wine producer early on in your holiday and come out with a case (12 bottles) or two to drink while you're on holiday. You don't have to buy a full case of the same wine.

The vast majority of the huge range of French wines have not been mentioned here. Not even all the best known regional wines have been named. The subject is huge and, in the end, comes down to taste. If a serious part of your holiday is to be spent savouring the fermented fruits of the vine, start early, don't automatically go for the cheapest (although no harm will come of it if you do), taste and enjoy. (See also Chapter 6, EATING AND DRINKING, for more on wine.)

BEER *(la bière)*

The normal French product, found in any supermarket, is a lager-type beer of about 4½% alcoholic strength. Kanterbrau, Kronenbourg and '33' are well known brands. Buy these in packs of 10 or 24 non-returnable bottles containing 25cl (½ pint), at around 2F the bottle, and serve cool. More expensive odd bottles from Britain, Ireland, Belgium and Germany can sometimes be found in big supermarkets.

SPIRITS *(les alcools)*

Unlike wine, spirits are heavily taxed and cost over three-quarters of the British price. And unlike French beer, you can even save a few pence by buying 'duty-free' whisky on the car-ferry. Otherwise there is nothing to report. You will find them all in the supermarket, with Scotch whisky in familiar brands. (Look carefully at the label if you see what appears to be a bargain whisky: it will probably be made in France, *fabriqué en France*, and watered down to 30% alcohol instead of the normal 40%. The alcoholic strength always figures on the label in the case of spirits, liqueurs and aperitifs.) Other spirits and the like are described in Chapter 6, EATING AND DRINKING.

TOBACCO *(tabac)*

Cigarettes and tobacco are not on sale in the supermarket. You have to go to a *tabac* shop, which often sells newspapers and postcards as well; if so, it will also be licensed to sell postage stamps *(timbres-poste)*, thereby saving you a wait in a long queue at the big post office. Heavy increases in tax on tobacco are promised for 1991, which may bring the well-known Gauloises Bleues (made of French tobacco) up to a shocking 7F per packet. (All packets hold 20.) Marlboro and other exotic brands may be up to twice that price.

CHAPTER EIGHT

MENUS AND RECIPES

If you are passionately devoted to cookery, a self-catering holiday in France will see you sitting pretty (well, not sitting, but shopping, chopping, stirring, tasting and perspiring). You will take a selection of your favourite books, wine- and gravy-stained and with your personal notes, and they will come home again to inspire your labours until next year.

This chapter has a different aim. The dishes here are what a carefree French person on holiday might serve up without blushing: simple, quick and authentic. They include ready-made dishes that local people might buy to warm up and eat at home. One or two are a bit more adventurous.

What a French person would consider a reasonably proper meal in such circumstances would consist of a starter (either an *entrée* or an *hors d'oeuvre*), a main dish, then a simple salad, just lettuce with a *vinaigrette* dressing (this is what *salade* means when you see it on a restaurant menu after the meat course; anything with oddments in it would appear as a first course), followed by a go at the cheese board, with a mere three or four of France's 300 or 400 cheeses on it, and lastly a pudding, *le dessert*. And there you are. An average French gourmet, knowing they are going to get only a scratch meal, will be quite happy with that, and freshly baked bread throughout, but no butter (except in Normandy). They'd like some well chilled dry white wine with the fish, if any, but won't expect a noble vintage; for the rest, a local *rosé*, chilled, or an ordinary red – in which it is quite all right to drop a few ice cubes. Afterwards, a small freshly made cup of coffee.

What you do when you haven't invited a French gourmet is your own affair. One of the starters, followed by a couple of local peaches, would suit us for a light lunch or supper in hot weather.

In the following pages we start by giving recipes for a few light, one-dish meals; suggested menus for more substantial meals and their recipes follow.

NOTE ON INGREDIENTS AND MEASUREMENTS

The ingredients are listed with their French translations and some of the common brand names, so that you know what to ask for or look for when you shop. Where the ingredient is something you will be buying specifically for the dish, such as '4 slices of ham' it is translated precisely, including quantities: '*quatre tranches de jambon*'. However, where the item is something you are likely to buy anyway, only its name is translated – so '1 garlic clove, finely chopped' is simply translated as '*ail*' (garlic).

When you go shopping, say '*Je voudrais. . .*' ('I'd like. . .') or '*Avez-vous. . .?*' ('Have you got. . .?') and the name of the thing. As you may know, the French for 'some' or 'any' is *du* with a masculine single noun, *de la* with a feminine singular noun, but *de l'* with either of those if the noun begins with a vowel or a silent 'h' – as in *de l'huile* (some/any oil). It's *des* with any noun in the plural.

Some of the recipes use a cup measurement, which you can take to be teacup-sized – containing between one third and one half a pint. The metric measurements are converted into imperial, but as a rough guide, 1 kilogram = just over 2lb, while 100 grams = about 4oz. With fluid measurements, 20fl oz = 1 pint, and 1 litre = 1¾ pints.

SALAD COURSE

A word about the simple *salade* that the French eat after the main course. You will without fail wash your leaves of lettuce and dry them – you don't want water in a *vinaigrette*, do you? Your house will undoubtedly have either a wire basket (take the washed lettuce outdoors in it, and whirl it around) or salad spinner. Equally unfailingly, you will make your *vinaigrette* with five parts of the best olive oil, one part of good wine vinegar and a little salt and pepper. Some people add a little French mustard, the heretics. Mix that lot up just before serving, and fling it on the lettuce.

At the greengrocer's stall, *une salade* means a lettuce (or a substitute, such as endive, in winter). There are dozens of sorts of lettuce, all with different names, but the word *salade* covers the lot.

1 lettuce	*une salade*
4 or 5 parts good olive oil	*huile d'olive provençale, extra vièrge, première pression à froid*
1 part wine vinegar	*vinaigre de vin*
salt, pepper	*sel, poivre*

CHEESE COURSE

Books have been written about French cheeses. Buy small quantities lavishly. To be authentic, don't serve butter with it (except with Roquefort when it's strong), nor biscuits – bread is the thing. Children might prefer a fruit-flavoured yoghurt (*yaourt*), or a *petit suisse* (cream cheese) with a teaspoon of sugar and a dribble of red wine on it.

DESSERT

Here you will not need to cook: there's fresh fruit galore, *éclairs* and other freshly made pastries bought that day at the *pâtisserie*, or ice cream. There's an almost infinite variety of *glâces* (ice cream), with no non-milk fats allowed, so a little less cheap than the British product – and *sorbets* (real fruit water ices) in the supermarket. They are usually sold in 1 litre (1¾ pt) containers, rather too much for a small party at one sitting. All *gîtes* must have a fridge, but you will only be able to stock up if it has a frozen-food compartment. At your local *pâtisserie* or *confiserie* you might find real home-made ice cream (ingredients: egg yolk, cream, fresh fruit) at a luxury price.

You don't need a shopping list for fruit, just a shopping bag. For *pâtisserie* you need someone to carry the box, carefully and flat. For ice cream at the supermarket (Gervais seems a very good brand, with dozens of unusual flavours) you may need an insulated bag or box to bring it home.

Bon appétit!

LIGHT MEALS

CHARCUTERIE

Charcuterie

selection of *pâtés*, ham, cold sausage, etc. for 4	*une sélection de charcuterie pour quatre personnes*
bread	*pain*

A great big plate covered with slices of salami-type sausage (*saucisson sec*), *pâté* in variety, two or three kinds of ham, *rillettes*, and local specialities ('*Quelles sont les spécialités de la région?*' – 'What are the specialities of the region?'). Since you don't want a lot of each, rather small amounts of a wide selection – for sampling, picking and choosing (and anyway, it's dull to buy plastic wrapped factory-made products from supermarket shelves) – go to the specialist shop, *la charcuterie* (that's the shop and the stuff it sells) and ask for '*une sélection de charcuterie pour quatre personnes*' (a selection of *charcuterie* for four people). This would probably be enough to feed five or six for starters and will make a good cold lunch for four people. It is worth adding '*c'est pour manger froid*' ('it's for eating cold'), as some of the shop's products, such as certain sausages, need warming or cooking.

Be adventurous! Something you've never seen or heard of before might turn out to be delicious, and then you can go back next day and buy a lot of it. Every region of France is different when it comes to *charcuterie*, and each shop is different too. Serve it with fresh bread from the *boulangerie* (bakery) next door, ordinary red table wine (*vin ordinaire* or *vin de table*) and perhaps salad, if it is to be a meal. You'll find that you won't need butter – there are enough fats in the meats already. *(Serves 4)*

TOMATES FARCIES CHAUDES
Hot baked stuffed tomatoes

*If you don't feel like making these yourself, get them
ready-cooked from the traiteur (sort of grocer) – the French
often do. Buy them shortly before eating, and heat them up
in the oven. Stuffings vary from traiteur to traiteur, but
usually include sausage meat or minced beef, seasoned and
cooked with herbs. Ask for quatres tomates farcies.
If you feel like baking them yourself, buy big knobbly
baking tomatoes, sometimes called tomates marmandes,
which are so large that four weigh 1kg (2lb).*

4 large baking tomatoes	*quatre tomates pour farcir*
500g (1lb) sausage meat or minced beef	*une livre de chair à saucisse ou de bifteck haché*
2 tablespoons chopped parsley	*persil*
1 teaspoon chopped sage or savory or 2 teaspoons thyme (or wild thyme)	*sauge ou sarriette ou thym ou serpolet*
salt, pepper	*sel, poivre*

Heat the oven to 200°C (400°F, gas 6). Slice the tops off the
tomatoes and scoop out the centres, seeds and juice with a
spoon. Mix the sausage meat or mince with the herbs in a
bowl and season generously. Season inside the tomatoes and
divide the mixture between them. Stand in a greased dish and
bake for about an hour until soft. Serve with bread and a
green salad. *(Serves 4)*

OEUFS A LA TRIPES

Eggs in a creamy onion sauce

No, it's not tripe, but hard-boiled eggs cooked in the kind of creamy onion sauce favoured for tripe. The strips of egg white look a bit like tripe, too. You can buy ready-made stock in some supermarkets.

6 large eggs	*oeufs*
35g (1¼oz) butter	*beurre*
4 onions, sliced thinly	*oignons*
500ml (17fl oz) mixture of	*bouillon, bouillon-cubes*
stock and milk, or milk with	*lait*
½ stock cube dissolved in it	
1 bouquet garni	*un bouquet garni*
salt, pepper, cayenne	*sel, poivre, cayenne*
nutmeg	*muscade*

Hard-boil 6 eggs for 12 minutes, drain immediately and cover with cold water (to stop the yolks turning blue). Cook the sliced onions in the butter very gently until softened, stirring occasionally. Sprinkle with flour and cook, stirring for a minute, then add the stock and/or milk and cube and the bouquet garni. Bring back to the boil, stirring gently. Simmer for 10 minutes, then season with salt, pepper and a little cayenne and nutmeg. Peel the eggs and quarter lengthways. Remove the bouquet garni, add the eggs to the pan and heat through. Serve with bread. *(Serves 4)*

PAELLA

Paella

This is cheating, because it's a Spanish dish. But the French have taken to it in a moderately big way. Usually they don't make it at home because it's a lot of bother. Freshly cooked paella can be seen at the traiteur: bits of chicken, rings of squid, mussels, prawns and slices of spicy sausage in well flavoured yellow rice (the yellow should be from saffron, but it's probably turmeric). This is where you get what you pay for, or ought to; cheapish versions are not to be recommended. If you see a great pan arriving in the shop window, looking bright and appetizing, go to it. Don't forget that a portion for four may be enough for five or six.

ready-made paella for 4   *paella pour quatre personnes*

Spread the paella out in a flat dish and heat through in a low oven, covered with foil (*papier d'aluminium*) for 15 minutes. *(Serves 4)*

PATES FRAICHES

Fresh pasta with bought sauce

Pasta has been adopted by the French even more than by the British. As well as the usual dried sorts, the supermarket will have fresh pasta, pâtes fraîches, in plastic packs in the chill shelves, as you are probably familiar with from home. Fresh pasta is much tastier than the dried sort, and there are all kinds: simple noodles (nouilles), ravioli, and so on. Check on the 'sell by' date (date limite de vente). Don't bother making a sauce; there are quite good pasta sauces in jars made by Buitoni – sauce provençale is among the best. A 500g (1lb) jar of a tomato-based sauce will feed four, as will a smaller 300g (11oz) jar of a herb-based sauce like

137

pesto. (In the supermarket freezers you'll find some useful complete pasta dishes – lasagne, stuffed cannelloni and that sort of thing).

500g (1lb) fresh pasta	*une livre de pâtes fraîches*
pasta sauce for 4	*sauce de pâtes toute faite pour quatres personnes*
50g (2oz) grated Parmesan cheese	*parmesan rapé*

Heat the sauce in a pan, but do not boil. Cook the pasta in boiling, salted water for 2–3 minutes only (fresh pasta cooks much more quickly than dried). Drain the pasta, and put in a big bowl. Pour the sauce over the top and mix. Serve immediately, with a bowl of grated Parmesan cheese (the French would probably sprinkle grated Gruyère on top, but Parmesan is better). *(Serves 4)*

MOULES MARINIERES

Mussels cooked in white wine

If you've never had this delicious, inexpensive dish, try it first at a restaurant where you can see the natives devouring platefuls with gusto. It's easy to get it right, once you've seen and tasted it. Serve in soup-plates, with a lot of fresh, crusty bread (baguettes). You'll need a large, empty bowl for the shells, and a spoon for the juice – you can use the shell of your first mussels as tweezers to cut out the remainder.

The mussels you will find on sale are from carefully inspected mussel farms. Don't try collecting you own from the rocks; the pollution level may be low enough for safe bathing, but not for consuming in concentrated form.

This recipe is good with the nice little moules du bouchot from the Atlantic coast. Mediterranean ones from the Languedoc lagoons can sometimes be rather salty (well, not

the mussels, but the juice). In that case, start off with just
water in the pan. When most of the mussels have opened,
pour off the water and juice, add the wine, chopped parsley
and chopped shallots, and give them a minute longer.
Another idea is to add 125ml (4fl oz) crème fraîche (thick
cream) to the juice before you pour it over the mussels
on the plate.

4kg (9lb) mussels	*quatre kilos de moules*
500ml (17fl oz) dry white wine (4 glasses)	*vin blanc sec*
4 tablespoons parsley, finely chopped	*persil*
4 shallots, chopped	*échalotes*

Scrub and wash the mussels thoroughly, scraping off the
'beard'. Throw away any that are open or broken. Put the
white wine, chopped parsley and chopped shallots into your
biggest pan with the mussels. Cover tightly and bring rapidly
to the boil. Cook for about 3–4 minutes, clapping the lids on
tightly and shaking the top mussels to the bottom occasionally.
The mussels are cooked when all are open – don't cook for too
long or they will be tough. Some may obstinately refuse to
open, and should be discarded as they will not be good. Serve
the mussels piled high in soup-plates, with the juice from the
pan strained over them. You will need plates or a big bowl for
the discarded shells. *(Serves 4)*

RATATOUILLE

Provençal vegetable stew

*A delicious mix of vegetables that improves by standing for
24 hours before eating. Good hot or cold – serve with hearty
bread and follow with salad.*

2 medium aubergines	*aubergines*
½ kilo (1lb) courgettes	*une livre de courgettes*
3 shallots, or ½ onion	*échalotes, oignons*
1 green pepper	*un poivron vert*
2 red peppers	*deux poivrons rouges*
1 yellow pepper	*un poivron jaune*
700g (1½lb) ripe tomatoes	*un kilo de tomates mûres*
2 cloves garlic, thinly sliced	*ail*
olive oil	*huile d'olive*
salt, pepper	*sel, poivre*

Cut the aubergine into 2cm slices (a good ½ inch) and cut
each slice into halves or quarters. Sprinkle liberally with salt
and allow the juices to drain for half an hour. Chop the other
vegetables into large chunks (the tomatoes can be halved or
quartered, depending on size – remove the skin if you like).

Rinse the aubergine well to get off the excess salt, and pat
dry on kitchen paper or a clean cloth.

Pour a saucer-sized pool of olive oil into a large, thick-
bottomed pan. Soften the onion over medium heat, then add
the aubergine. Give it a good stir to distribute the oil, which
the aubergine will quickly soak up. Let the aubergine soften,
then add the other vegetables and garlic. Stir the vegetables
now and then, to prevent them sticking, until their juices
begin to flow. Add a liberal helping of black pepper and a
little salt (add more later, to taste), and let it cook gently for
45 minutes or so. Keep the pan covered to retain the juice
while cooking (any excess can be boiled off right at the end).
Leave to stand for a day if you can, as the flavours then
develop beautifully. Serve reheated or cold. *(Serves 4)*

MENUS

Melon with port
Stew served with lettuce or *chicorée frisée*
Palmiers, sweet biscuits or plain fruit

A very quick menu, using all bought ingredients, but substantial and very French.

MELON AU PORTO

Melon with port

Use the small round cantaloup or charentais melons, not the larger rugby-football-shaped yellow ones, nor the big green watermelons with red flesh and black seeds (though slices of these are good at any time when you're hot and thirsty). Cantaloup or charentais melons are sweet with rosy flesh, but the French serve them as a first course.

Although this dish is often made with red port, white port is more common in France. If you use white port, you could drink the rest of the bottle as an aperitif. As an alternative, you can use any sweet muscat wine – for example, Muscat de Frontignan; it's cheaper than the better-known Muscat de Beaumes-de-Venise.

2 cantaloup or charentais melons	*deux melons, cantaloup ou charantais*
Port	*porto*

Cut the melons in half, scoop out the seeds and pour a good couple of tablespoons of port into the hollow – or fill the hollow completely, if you wish. *(Serves 4)*

RAGOUT

Stew

Stew is a libellous word for some of the glories of *la cuisine française*: meat or poultry simmered for hours, often in wine (teetotallers should note that all the alcohol evaporates early in the process if it's not flamed off at the start), with a variety of traditional additions for flavour and consistency. *Boeuf bourguignon, boeuf en daube, lapin chasseur*; they all take time and trouble. But it's not much more fuss and bother to make these dishes for ten people than for two. And if you've got big enough pots, they're all the better if you make them for 50.

Such stews, therefore, are among the most successful products of a good *traiteur* (type of grocer). The local butcher might make some, too. Look for big bowls or pans of chunks of meat or poultry in gravy (which might be in a jellified state when cold). A portion won't be cheap. Similar dishes in cans are less expensive but less good (more carrots than beef, or other cost-cutting substitutions). There's also a recipe for *coq au vin* in this section.

We give no shopping list; there is a bewildering variety of names for the long-cooked dishes, every region has its own specialities, and no two *traiteurs* do things the same way. If you're new to the town and you see a fairly pricey shop with customers who look as if they know what's what, you're on the track. Ask *'Avez-vous un ragoût à emporter et à réchauffer?'* ('Do you have a ready-made casserole or stew for reheating?')

Your purchase should be warmed through in a saucepan and served with, perhaps, boiled potatoes or good bread, used to mop up the last drop of luscious gravy. Green salad is good, too; the French often put lettuce leaves into the last of the gravy. *(Serves 4)*

Frogs' legs
Soft tomato omelette with green bean salad
Normandy apple or pear tart (nothing too creamy)

CUISSES DE GRENOUILLES

Frogs' legs

*Well, you might as well give these a try just once. There's
nothing horrid about them, and many small French children
find them fun. Serve them with fresh, crusty bread. Just
suck the flesh off the tiny bones to eat them; it doesn't taste
of anything, really, except garlic and parsley. Expensive per
ounce of protein. Don't go frog-hunting; in the supermarket
you'll see deep-frozen frogs' legs, ready to cook, and
imported from Romania or Thailand or somewhere – it's
only in expensive restaurants in Burgundy that you'll meet
the plump thighs of a genuine fresh French frog.*

400–600g (14–20oz) frozen frogs' legs	*cuisses de grenouilles congelées*
3 tablespoons flour	*farine*
8–12 tablespoons olive oil	*huile d'olive*
115–170g (4–6oz) butter	*beurre*
2 garlic cloves, finely chopped	*ail*
3 tablespoons chopped parsley	*persil*
salt, pepper	*sel, poivre*

Defrost the frogs' legs thoroughly and separate them. They
are long and thin, so bend the knees to make oval shapes.
Dust them with seasoned flour. Heat equal quantities of
butter and oil together, using a second pan if necessary, and
cook the frogs' legs until golden brown. Move to a serving
plate, toss the garlic in the butter and sprinkle this, with some

of the juices, over the frogs' legs. Sprinkle with parsley and serve. *(Serves 4)*

PIPERADE

Soft tomato omelette

This is a Basque speciality. In Basque country the ham would be the excellent raw jambon de Bayonne, but ordinary cooked ham does well enough. There should be about twice as much cooked vegetable as beaten egg.

4 slices of ham	*quatre tranches de jambon*
4 tablespoons olive oil	*huile d'olive*
1 onion	*oignons*
1 red sweet pepper	*un poivron rouge*
1 green pepper	*un poivron vert*
4 tomatoes	*quatre tomates*
2 garlic cloves, finely chopped	*ail*
8 eggs	*oeufs*
salt, pepper	*sel, poivre*

Heat some olive oil in a frying pan and cook the ham. When it is done, take it out of the pan and keep it warm. Slice the onion thinly, and cook it in the frying pan until soft. Slice the peppers, scald, peel and slice the tomatoes, discarding the seeds, crush the garlic, and add the whole lot to the frying pan, with salt and pepper. Stir occasionally. While the vegetables are cooking, break the eggs into a bowl and beat them. When the vegetables are soft, add the eggs. Do not overcook the eggs; aim at the consistency of soft scrambled egg. Put the ham slices on top, and serve. *(Serves 4)*

Pancakes filled with a creamy cheese sauce
Ham in a Madeira sauce with carrots
Ice cream or fruit sorbet

A filling menu based on ready-made food. The combination of ham and Madeira sauce is a French classic.

CREPES FOURREES AVEC UNE SAUCE AU FROMAGE

Pancakes filled with a creamy cheese sauce

There are several brands of these in the supermarket deep freeze, with different sauces in and over them. They usually contain 4 pancakes.

a packet of filled pancakes   *un paquet de crêpes fourrées*

Either defrost then reheat for 10 minutes in a greased dish in the oven, or reheat from frozen in a low oven for 30 minutes. *(Serves 4)*

JAMBON A LA SAUCE MADERE

Ham in Madeira sauce

You will be able to find tins of sauce madère, a sauce based on Madeira wine, in the supermarket. Liebig is a good brand. The slight sweetness of Madeira brings out the qualities of the ham. New carrots would go well with this; they respond to a sweet sauce.

4 thick slices of ham

200g (7oz) can of Madeira sauce

quatre tranches de jambon de York ou jambon de pays
une boîte de sauce madère

Lay the slices of ham into a greased ovenproof dish, and empty the can of Madeira sauce over the top. Heat through thoroughly in a fairly low oven for 10 minutes. *(Serves 4)*

Savoury *vol-au-vent*
Trout cooked in foil with braised fennel
Ice cream or fruit

BOUCHEES A LA REINE

Savoury *vol-au-vent*

*These are flaky pastry cases filled with oddments (mainly
chicken and mushrooms, or perhaps brains) in a creamy
sauce. The whole thing can be bought at the traiteur (grocer)
– 'Avez-vous des bouchées à la reine?' ('Have you any
bouchées à la reine?') – or you can buy freshly baked
vol-au-vent cases at the pâtisserie, and fill them yourself.
Quite decent canned filling can be bought in the
supermarket, but don't buy the cases there, as the
factory-made boxes of vol-au-vent cases are very dull
compared with the freshly-baked variety. Of course,
you can bake your own, using frozen puff pastry
(pâte feuilleté surgelé).*

from the pâtisserie:
4 empty *vol-au-vent* cases

*quatre vol-au-vents pour
garnir*

from the supermarket:
400g (14oz) can filling

*une boîte de garniture
pour bouchées à la reine*

Buy the *vol-au-vent* cases first so that you can judge how much
filling will be needed – pastry sizes vary from substantial to
tiny cocktail cases. Fill the cases and heat through in a
medium oven. *(Serves 4)*

TRUITE EN PAPILLOTE

Trout cooked in foil

The fishmonger will have inexpensive farmed trout, or you might buy some from the man selling live trout at the market (he brings them in a tank on his lorry, from his fish farm). Fennel (fenouil) is an especially good herb to use with fish, but you'll have to gather it yourself, as it is not readily available fresh. It has blue-green upright stalks and a yellow parasol-shaped head of buds and seeds. As a vegetable, braised fennel bulbs would go very nicely with this dish.
Slices of salmon are good cooked this way, too.

4 trout	*quatre truites*
butter or olive oil	*beurre ou huile d'olive*
1 lemon	*un citron*
herbs (parsley, thyme or marjoram)	*persil, thym ou marjolaine*
salt, pepper	*sel, poivre*

Gut the trout and wash inside. Cut pieces of aluminium foil (*papier d'aluminium*), large enough to wrap each fish in, and butter or oil them sparingly. Place the fish on the foil, season in the belly cavity with salt and pepper, add a lemon slice and a good teaspoon of chopped fresh herbs per fish. Fold the foil all around to make a water-tight parcel and put the fish in a pre-heated moderate oven at 180°C (350°F; gas 4) for about 20 minutes or until done. *(Serves 4)*

Tomato salad
Chicken in red wine with new potatoes
Sablé (*gâteau* made with shortbread dough) of some sort,
something crisp or fruit sorbet

A traditional salad followed by a very French casserole.

SALADE DE TOMATES

Tomato salad

*This is the same as salade niçoise (page 162) with the
oddments left out. But it's hardly worth making unless you
can get fresh basil (it's not an oddment, but essential with
tomatoes) and the flavourful, bumpy sort of tomatoes.*

700g (1½lb) tomatoes	*un kilo de tomates*
½ large Spanish onion	*un oignon doux*
fresh basil leaves	*du basilic frais*
sugar	*sucre*
1½ tablespoons white wine vinegar	*vinaigre de vin blanc*
6–8 tablespoons olive oil	*huile d'olive*
salt, pepper	*sel, poivre*

Scald, peel and slice the tomatoes, discarding the seeds, any
hard parts and juice. Peel the onion and cut it into thin rings.
Arrange the slices of tomato and onion in a shallow bowl in
layers, seasoning and sprinkling each layer liberally with
chopped basil as you go. Add a little sugar and a drop of
vinegar on top, then pour over the olive oil. Be lavish with the
oil; you can mop it up with bread. (*Serves 4*)

151

COQ AU VIN

Chicken in red wine

*The coq of the original recipe was a large, mature bird, and
the old-fashioned way of cooking it was to marinate it in the
wine for 24 hours and to add its blood to the final dish.
You can skip these two stages! Nevertheless, a large,
good-quality bird is needed and this will be expensive.
Fried triangles of toast or bread are traditionally good with
this dish, and a green salad goes well.
Buy your chicken from the supermarket – poulet fermier is a
free-range chicken (Loué is a good label), and one that is
ready for the oven is poulet prêt-à-cuire (or p.à.c.).
A specialist chicken shop often supplies the bird with head,
feet and most of the innards intact; if you ask for it to be
prêt-à-cuire they will prepare it, asking you which of the
oddments – they all have their uses – you want. You can use
them to make stock. You can also buy stock (bouillon)
ready-made in some supermarkets, or could use stock cubes
(bouillon-cubes).*

2kg (4¼lb) chicken	*un poulet fermier de deux kilos*
3 tablespoons flour	*farine*
2 tablespoons olive oil	*huile d'olive*
40g (1½oz) butter	*beurre*
750ml (1¼pt) bottle full-bodied red wine, like Côtes du Rhône	*une bouteille de Côtes du Rhône*
2 onions, chopped	*oignons*
100g (4oz) bacon cubes	*cent grammes de lardons*
2 celery stalks, chopped	*céleri en branches*
4 tablespoons brandy for flaming	*cognac*
40ml (14fl oz) chicken stock	*bouillon de poulet*
bouquet garni	*bouquet garni*
1 tablespoon tomato paste	*concentré de tomates*

12–18 pickling onions	*petits oignons*
250g (8oz) button	*champignons de Paris*
mushrooms quartered if large	
salt, pepper	*sel, poivre*
carrots, potatoes	*carottes, pommes de terre*

Take out the wishbone and cut the chicken into 6 pieces: 2 legs, 2 wings (each taking a good end of the breast) and 2 breasts. Cut out the backbone, but keep it, with the two wing tips. Season the chicken pieces with salt and pepper and dust with flour. In a flameproof casserole big enough to hold the chicken, heat 1 tablespoon each of oil and butter. Put in the chicken pieces and fry gently on all sides for 20 minutes until golden. Meanwhile, boil the wine in a pan until it is reduced by half. Heat 1 tablespoon each of oil and butter in a frying pan and fry the chopped onion with the bacon and celery slowly until soft.

When the chicken is golden, spoon all fat from the casserole. Warm the brandy in a ladle. Stand back and set it alight. Pour it over the chicken, spooning it back over the top while it continues to burn. Tuck the backbone and wingtips in and add the bacon, onions and celery to the casserole, leaving the fat. Add the reduced wine to the casserole with the stock, bouquet garni and tomato paste. Cover and simmer gently for 30 minutes.

Put the pickling onions in the frying pan and fry gently, tossing occasionally, until coloured. Add them to the casserole. Gently toss the mushroom caps in the frying pan.

When the chicken is ready, discard the backbone and wing tips and check that the liquid has reduced to about 300ml (9fl oz) (boil it down, if necessary). Mash together about 1 tablespoon butter and 1 tablespoon of flour. Add this to the casserole in pea-sized bits, stirring until the sauce is thickened. Check the seasonings and stir in the mushrooms. Sprinkle with parsley and serve with boiled carrots and/or potatoes. *(Serves 6)*

Leek soup
Slices of veal in cream with peas or braised celery

This is a light menu.

SOUPE AUX POIREAUX

Leek soup

*A pleasant, light soup that includes both the white and the
green parts of the leek. It's worth making double the
quantity and serving the rest chilled – as vichyssoise, it's the
perfect soup for hot weather. You can buy stock (bouillon)
ready-made in some supermarkets, but if you can't find any,
use stock cubes (bouillon-cubes).*

500g (1lb) leeks	*une livre de poireaux*
1 tablespoon olive oil	*huile d'olive*
3 tablespoons butter	*beurre*
500g (1lb) potatoes	*une livre de pommes de terre*
2 garlic cloves, finely chopped	*ail*
750ml (1¼pt) stock or stock cubes	*bouillon ou bouillon-cubes*
chopped chives or chervil	*ciboulette ou cerfeuil*
salt, pepper	*sel, poivre*

Split the leeks and wash well. Cut into rings and cook these in
a large saucepan in the oil and butter for 5 minutes over high
heat. Add the potatoes, garlic, stock and herbs and simmer
for 20 minutes. Season well, breaking up the vegetables with a
wooden spoon.

To eat cold, seive or purée in a blender, then stir in about
125ml (4fl oz) *crème fraîche*. Serve very cold, sprinkled with
chopped chives. *(Serves 4)*

ESCALOPES DE VEAU A LA CREME

Slices of veal in cream

*Ask the butcher for some escalopes (thin slices) of veal.
If you go to the trouble of coating them with egg and
breadcrumbs (chapelure), then frying them, you've got
Wiener schnitzel. The French prefer them à la crème, using
crème fraîche, a thick cream that has been slightly fermented
to give a nutty taste. It's an essential ingredient for French
cooking – you can't miss it, near the yoghurts in the dairy
section of the supermarket.
A chilled rosé wine goes well with this. For vegetables, try
peas or braised celery.*

4 escalopes of veal	*quatre escalopes de veau*
2 tablespoons olive oil	*huile d'olive*
25g (1oz) butter	*beurre*
2 tablespoons white wine	*vin blanc*
200ml (7fl oz) thick cream	*un pot de crème fraîche*

Season the escalopes and fry them in a little oil and butter
until they are cooked, then remove and keep warm. Pour the
white wine (some people use a sweet white wine, or white
vermouth, or brandy – go on, experiment!) into the pan, turn
up the heat and let it bubble and reduce while you scrape the
bottom of the pan. Season, then add several dollops of *crème
fraîche* (not *crème liquide*, also sold in the supermarket). Let
the cream bubble up too, and reduce a bit. Pour over the
escalopes.

To make an inferior but cheaper dish, use *escalopes de
dinde*, slices of breast from a (battery) turkey. Or buy a piece
of pork tenderloin (*filet mignon de porc*) and slice it into a lot
of tiny escalopes. *(Serves 4)*

Red pepper salad
Black pudding with apples
Very smelly cheese

SALADE DE POIVRONS ROUGES

Red pepper salad

Most herbs are good with this salad, but if you do not have any to hand, parsley will do just as well. The broad-leaved sort has more flavour than the curly sort.

2 large red peppers	*deux poivrons rouges*
flat parsley and/or	*persil, thym*
other herbs, such as thyme	
6 tablespoons good olive oil	*huile d'olive*
salt, pepper	*sel, poivre*

Hold the peppers on a carving fork over a naked gas flame and char the skin. Scrape off most of the blackened skin (no need to be too fussy) and cut the flesh into strips, discarding the seeds. Put the strips into a shallow dish, scatter with the chopped fresh herbs, and season. Pour olive oil lavishly over the salad and leave for an hour or two (or store for a day in the fridge) before eating. *(Serves 4)*

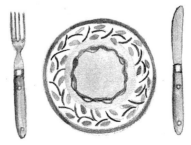

BOUDIN NOIR AUX POMMES

Black pudding with apples

You perhaps disdain black puddings in Britain, and you may be right (though a few British butchers make their own, delicious ones). French boudins are different, and well worth trying. As with so many things in this individualistic country, they differ significantly from region to region (around Limoges they are made with chestnut flour – boudins à la châtaigne – super!) and from butcher to butcher. If you like black pudding, why not try several butchers, and have a 'which boudin?' session. You'll need about 100–150g (4–5oz) per person.
Slightly sharp apples, such as reinettes, are best for this dish. The golden ones are too bland. On menus, apples in main courses are often called pommes fruit, to distinguish them from pommes de terre (potatoes), which are often shortened to just pommes, as in pommes frites (chips).

1–2 black puddings, depending on size	*boudin noir pour quatre personnes*
3 tablespoons olive oil	*huile d'olive*
30g (1oz) butter	*beurre*
500kg (1lb) potatoes	*une livre de pommes de terre*
4 apples	*quatre pommes*
salt, pepper	*sel, poivre*

Slice the black pudding(s) and fry gently in butter and oil, turning once. Cook the sliced potatoes in salted water. Core the apples and slice into rings. Fry these in 1 tablespoon each oil and butter, turning once. Arrange the potato slices in a hot dish, seasoning them well. Put the black pudding on top and garnish with apple slices. *(Serves 4)*

Cooked courgette salad
Poached sausage with hot potato salad
Medium cheese, such as Pont l'Evêque

COURGETTES A LA GREQUE

Cooked courgette salad

Salads of cooked vegetables are popular in France and extend the choice in hot weather. This is a light salad that can be prepared and left in the fridge while you go out for the day.

1 onion, chopped	*oignons*
3 tablespoons olive oil	*huile d'olive*
1 garlic clove, finely chopped	*ail*
150ml (5fl oz) dry white wine	*vin blanc sec*
2 tablespoons tomato paste	*concentré de tomates*
1 teaspoon coriander seeds, crushed	*coriandre*
600g (1¼lb) courgettes, trimmed	*un kilo de courgettes*
lemon juice	*jus de citron*
chopped parsley to serve	*persil*
salt, pepper	*sel, poivre*

Heat the olive oil in a saucepan and fry the onion until soft, then add the garlic, white wine, tomato paste and coriander seeds. Season and simmer for 2 minutes. Meanwhile, halve the courgettes across then lengthways, then cut into sticks. Add them to the pan with just enough water to cover. Bring them to the boil, then cover and simmer for 10 minutes. Leave them in the pan until cold, then remove with a slotted spoon, leaving the liquid. Serve the courgettes dressed with lemon juice and a little olive oil, and parsley.

The bouillon left over can be used to make another salad of the same sort. Slice carrots into the liquid, cook for about 5 minutes and serve in the same way. *(Serves 4)*

SAUCISSE AVEC SALADE TIEDE
DE POMMES DE TERRE

Poached sausage with hot potato salad

You can buy une saucisse à cuire (a sausage for cooking) or
a chunk of one from the charcuterie. It resembles a giant
frankfurter, and is for heating through in boiling water,
rather different from the ordinary grilling sausage, saucisse
de Toulouse, which can be seen in long coils. When buying
the potatoes, look for the yellow-fleshed, waxy ones –
Roseval is a good variety.

500g (1lb) cooking sausage	*saucisse à cuire*
400ml (4fl oz) cheap white wine	*vin blanc*
500g (1lb) potatoes	*pommes de terre*
salt, pepper	*sel, poivre*
parsley	*persil*

VINAIGRETTE

2 tablespoons vinegar	*vinaigre*
4 tablespoons olive oil	*huile d'olive*
salt, pepper	*sel, poivre*

Put the sausage in a pan and cover it with water or equal parts
water and wine. Simmer over very low heat for half an hour
or more (the longer it is cooked, the more fat will be
removed). Boil the potatoes until cooked. To serve, slice the
hot potatoes and hot sausage and arrange them in a shallow
bowl. Pour over a good vinaigrette (here you can be heavy-
handed with the vinegar), and scatter chopped parsley over
the top. *(Serves 4)*

159

Green beans with bacon
Tuna with capers
Camembert cheese

HARICOTS VERTS AUX LARDONS

Green beans with bacon pieces

Tiny slim green beans need no more than bringing back to the boil in salted water, and can then be served dressed with good olive oil, or be reheated with a couple of spoonfuls each of butter and water. Bigger beans, with round haricots visible inside, need more substantial cooking. You'll probably find that 400g (12oz) is enough for four, but as you will have to buy half a kilo, you might as well cook them all and use any left over in a salad. Lardons (bacon pieces) are sold vacuum-packed in the supermarket.

500g (1lb) large green beans	*une livre de haricots verts*
100g (4oz) bacon pieces	*cent grammes de lardons*
2 shallots, chopped	*échalotes*
1 tablespoon butter	*beurre*
1 tablespoon olive oil	*huile d'olive*
parsley	*persil*
salt, pepper	*sel, poivre*

Cook the trimmed, halved beans in plenty of boiling salted water for 10 minutes. At the same time, fry the *lardons* in butter and oil in a flameproof casserole with the shallots. Drain the beans, toss in the fat from the *lardons* and the butter, season with pepper only (you'll find that the *lardons* are pretty salty already) and sprinkle a little parsley on top. *(Serves 4–5)*

THON AUX CAPRES

Tuna with capers

You will see whacking great specimens of tuna fish in the market (you may see bonito too; its texture is less close and heavy than tuna). It is usually cut into one great steak from the tail, or a belly piece (this is best) with no bones. Capers (câpres) can be bought in small jars in the supermarket.

700g (1½lb) tuna, in one or two pieces	*une ou deux tranches de thon, sept cents grammes maximum*
2 tablespoons olive oil	*huile d'olive*
500g (1lb) tomatoes	*une livre de tomates*
1 lemon	*un citron*
1 tablespoon capers	*câpres*
125–150ml (4–5fl oz) white wine	*vin blanc*
salt, pepper	*sel, poivre*

Cut the tuna into thick slices, and fry gently in a very little oil. When you have slightly browned both sides, add slices of tomato, a good squeeze of lemon, a few capers, season and moisten with white wine. Cover with a lid and cook over very low heat for 20–30 minutes, until the flesh is tender and comes off the bone. Check occasionally that the liquid is not evaporating too fast. *(Serves 4)*

Salad with tuna, eggs, tomatoes and olives
Chicken in aspic with lettuce *chiffonade*
Pastry with *crème pâtissière*

A lovely classic salad menu for a hot night or a long, lazy lunch. The tuna makes a nice balance against the chicken.

SALADE NIÇOISE

Salad with tuna, eggs, tomatoes and olives

This mixed salad traditionally comes from the region around Nice, but is served almost everywhere in France. Try shopping in the market for your tomatoes; you'll probably find one of the varieties gourmets love – irregular bumpy shapes with real flavour and not much water. Salade niçoise can be bought ready-made at le traiteur (the grocer), but it might be unclassical, with bits of cold boiled potato, cooked French beans, or anything else, in it. These could be added to make a main course. This is the authentic version (or one of them).

2 eggs	*oeufs*
600g (1¼lb) tomatoes	*six cents grammes de tomates*
1 green pepper	*un poivron vert*
12–16 black olives	*olives noires*
10 fresh basil leaves	*basilic frais*
200g (7oz) can of tuna or 50g (2oz) can anchovy fillets	*une boîte de thon ou une petite boîte de filets d'anchois*
5–6 tablespoons olive oil or *vinaigrette* (page 132)	*huile d'olive*
salt, pepper	*sel, poivre*

Hard-boil the eggs and leave on one side until you are ready to use them. Scald, peel and slice the tomatoes, discarding the seeds, any hard parts and juice. Slice the hard-boiled eggs; slice the peppers finely and discard the seeds. Either stone the olives and cut them in half, or warn the family: many a tooth has been broken on an olive stone. Line a shallow bowl with slices of tomato, season and sprinkle liberally with chopped basil. Then arrange over them, in layers, the slices of hard-boiled egg and pepper, and anchovies if you are using them. Season the layers as you go. If you are using tuna, scatter large chunks over the top. Season, sprinkle with basil and pour over the olive oil or *vinaigrette*. *(Serves 4)*

POULET EN GELEE

Chicken in aspic

There are a hundred other things to do with a chicken, of course: a plain, roasted, free-range bird, especially if you put a lump of butter and a handful of fresh tarragon inside, is not to be sneezed at. Alternatively, somewhat overcooked, spit-roasted, battery birds can be seen rotating outside many butchers, ready to be whisked home and eaten straight away. But this is a good cold dish for a heat wave. If you wish, keep the breasts for a separate dish; they do nicely, for two people, as escalopes à la crème (page 155). Otherwise a 1.25kg (2½lb) chicken will do nicely.

1 chicken	*un poulet fermier prêt-à-cuire*
1 onion	*oignons*
tarragon	*estragon*
1 lemon	*un citron*
200ml (7fl oz) dry white wine	*vin blanc sec*
parsley	*persil*
chives	*ciboulette*
salt, pepper	*sel, poivre*

163

Chop the chicken into eight or ten joints and pack into a saucepan. Chop the onion and add to the pan. Barely cover the bird with water and bring to the boil. Cover the pan and simmer very gently for 30 minutes, then take it off the heat and allow to cool. Leaving the liquid in the pan, take out the joints. Remove all the meat from the bones and put it in a shallow bowl in the fridge. Chop the tarragon and add it to the pan with the bones and skin, the juice of the lemon and enough dry white wine to cover the whole lot generously. Bring to the boil and simmer (covered) for as long as you can spare the time (at least 30 minutes). Let it cool, then strain the liquid over the chicken pieces. Chop the parsley and chives and sprinkle over the top. Cover the bowl with cling film or a plate, and leave in the fridge overnight. By morning the whole thing will have jellied. Serve it with lettuce *chiffonade* – roll up the lettuce leaves and cut across to form ribbons. *(Serves 4)*

Oysters
Steak or sausage with ratatouille
Grapes

HUITRES

Oysters

*If you've never eaten an oyster in your life, why not try
some at a restaurant or buy some from a fishmonger in
Britain before you go? It's a three-to-one chance that you'll
find them delicious. They'll cost you a bomb, but when you
get to France, where the natives slurp down millions every
month (including those without an 'R'), you'll find they are
much less expensive. Having said that, prices and seasons
vary from region to region, so check before you buy. In
1990, oysters from our local fishmonger were usually costing
about 15F (£1.50) for 1kg (2lb), for which you got 10
whoppers or 18 small ones; he charges 20F (£2) for 1kg
(2lb), but for that he will open them with a practised flick of
the wrist and present them on a polystyrene platter covered
with shaved ice, and a lemon in the middle.*
*One should beware of oysters in some foreign countries, but
French ones are safe, whether they're bred on the shores of
the Atlantic or the Mediterranean (the industry is important
and the authorities are meticulous). Oysters are best with a
bottle of chilled dry white wine, but you can also try them
with Guinness, an old British habit in the days when oysters
were cheap at home. (You can find Guinness in some
supermarkets, where it is cheaper than in the UK.)*

1kg (2lb) oysters	*un kilo d'huîtres*
rye bread	*pain de seigle*
butter	*beurre*
2 lemons	*deux citrons*
ice, crushed	

Chill the wine, cut the rye bread into thin slices and butter it, and cut the lemons in half. Spread a layer of crushed ice on a tray. Open the oysters – perhaps the fishmonger or oyster merchant will give you a lesson, or even open them for you if you're eating them immediately. If not the classic method is to stick a short, blunt knife through the hinge, where the join is easy to see. There is now a patent gadget on sale that breaks the lip and goes in at the big end. Serve the oysters on the crushed ice and eat them with a squeeze of lemon, bread and butter. *(Serves 4)*

STEAK OU SAUCISSE AVEC RATATOUILLE

Steak or sausage with ratatouille

Both a plain grilled steak or a length of grilled saucisse de Toulouse (made in a long coil, 100% pork, with largeish chunks of lean and fat) go well with ratatouille, a wonderful provençal vegetable stew that uses up the August glut of tomatoes, courgettes, sweet peppers and aubergines.
The ratatouille recipe appears earlier, but you don't have to make your own, as it is good bought tinned or in frozen packets, and heated.
(See SHOPPING FOR FOOD, Chapter 7, for steak.)

4 steaks or 600–700g (1¼–1½lb) Toulouse sausage	*quatres steaks ou saucisse de Toulouse*
2 tablespoons butter	*beurre*
2 400g (14oz) cans of ratatouille or the recipe (page 142)	*deux boîtes de ratatouille*
salt, pepper	*sel, poivre*

Salt and pepper the steaks, put ½ tablespoon butter on each one and grill for 2–3 minutes each side. The saucisse will take about 15 minutes under the grill, turning it. Empty the ratatouille into a saucepan and heat thoroughly. *(Serves 4)*

Wilted lettuce with bacon
Lentils with grilled fattened duck breasts
Peaches

This whole menu comes from the south of France.

SALADE AUX LARDONS

Wilted lettuce with bacon

This salad often includes the gizzards (gésiers) of chicken, and the tiny fillet that separates from the back of duck or chicken breasts. The lardons are salty enough for the whole salad.

1 lettuce	*une laitue ou une salade*
100g (4oz) bacon pieces	*cent grammes de lardons*
1 tablespoon oil	*huile d'olive*
1 tablespoon wine vinegar	*vinaigre de vin*

Wash and dry the lettuce and arrange on 4 plates. Fry the lardons in the oil until they give off all their fat. Add the vinegar and bring to the boil over high heat. Throw over the lettuce, distributing the *lardons* evenly, and serve at once. *(Serves 4)*

LENTILLES

Lentils

A common reaction is 'Lentils? How dull!' They are despised and neglected in England, but deservedly esteemed in France – not the mushy yellow or red sort, but the little grey-green ones. You'll see them in plastic bags in the supermarket, labelled lentilles du Puy (the area around Le

Puy is where the best lentils are grown). They retain their shape in cooking, and have a pleasant nutty taste. Traditionally they accompany sausage, but can go with other meats. As they take a long time to cook, they're not ideal holiday food – unless you cut corners by using canned ones, which do very well. You will see cans of tarted-up lentils in the supermarket, notably lentilles cuisinées à la graisse d'oie (lentils cooked in goose fat). It's better to do your own improving. Serve with grilled chitterling sausages (andouillettes) or duck breasts (see below).

You won't be able to buy just one bay leaf, but you can perhaps pick one somewhere. We give the name, in case you're asking around in your search, because the laurier sauce (bay) isn't the laurier of the shrubbery. That's laurel, which is poisonous.

800g (1lb 14oz) can of green cooked lentils	une boîte de lentilles au naturel
1 onion	oignons
2 carrots	deux carottes
1 tablespoon olive oil or butter or pork fat	huile d'olive ou beurre ou saindoux
1 bay leaf	une feuille de laurier sauce
1 orange	une orange

Open the can of lentils and pour off the liquid. Slice the onion and carrots thinly, and cook them in a saucepan in the oil, butter or pork fat until soft. Add the lentils, bay leaf and the juice of an orange, cover and cook slowly for 15 minutes. (Serves 4)

MAGRETS GRILLES

Grilled fattened duck breasts

In Gascony, where Puy lentils are grown, grey ducks are fattened for foie gras. They also put great weight on the breasts, which are the true magrets de canard (duck steaks or cutlets). Like beef steaks, they are best cooked fast, sliced thin and eaten rare. Lentils make the classic partner.

2 fattened duck breasts, 250–300g (8–11oz) each	*deux magrets de canard*
salt, pepper	*sel, poivre*

Criss-cross the fat on the breasts with a sharp knife and rub salt and pepper into the fat and the lean. Grill on foil (*papier d'aluminium*) fat side up for 5 minutes, then turn and spoon a little fat over the lean. Grill for 5 minutes. Finish with a further 2 minutes on the fat side. Slice thinly and fan the meat out on top of the lentils, pouring the juices over the dish. *(Serves 4)*

Melon with raw cured ham
Mustardy rabbit
Light *pâtisserie*

MELON AU JAMBON CRU

Melon with raw cured ham

You can buy paper-thin slices of raw cured ham (jambon cru) from the local charcuterie (delicatessen). If you feel like having a break from melon, fresh figs (figues) are also delicious with this ham.

2 cantaloup or charentais melons
70g (3oz) raw cured ham, thinly sliced

deux melons, cantaloup ou charantais
soixante-dix grammes de jambon cru en tranches fines

Quarter the melons lengthways, peel and discard the skin. Cut the flesh into half-moon slices, arrange the slices of melon and ham on 4 plates, and serve. *(Serves 4)*

LAPIN A LA MOUTARDE

Mustardy rabbit

This is a very popular traditional dish. The quantity of mustard sounds enormous, but it's mild French mustard and the final result is pleasantly unagressive. Ready-prepared 'farmed' rabbits can be bought in the supermarket – you won't see 'wild' rabbits there, except in fur and in the deep freeze, imported from England. For fewer people, rabbit halves should be on sale in the supermarket; reduce the other ingredients accordingly. Plain boiled potatoes go well with

*this dish, as do cooked white haricot beans or peas stewed
with lettuce and onions.*

1 rabbit	*un lapin*
150g (5oz) jar Dijon mustard	*un pot de moutarde de Dijon*
150g (5oz) thick cream	*un pot de crème fraîche*
salt, pepper	*sel, poivre*

Place the rabbit in a roasting dish and smear the entire
contents of the mustard jar all over it. Place it in a pre-heated
oven at 225°C (440°F, gas 7) for 45–60 minutes until cooked.
Remove the cooked rabbit from the roasting dish, leaving the
juice, and put it on a serving dish to keep warm. A rabbit is
tricky to carve, so you may find it easier to cut it into portions
at this stage (2 back legs, saddle, 2 front legs plus some of the
ribs). Add the *crème fraîche* to the roasting dish and heat it
on top of the stove, scraping and stirring until the cream is
bubbling and well mixed with the juices. Season to taste.
Pour the resulting sauce into a sauce boat or bowl, and serve.
(Serves 4–5)

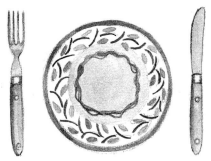

Tomatoes stuffed with tuna
Fried calf's liver with chopped spinach and fried bread triangles
Light *pâtisserie*

TOMATES AU THON

Tomatoes stuffed with tuna

This is for when you see enormous tomatoes on sale. Ideally you should make your own mayonnaise (all it needs is egg yolk, olive oil, care and experience), but you are on holiday, after all! There's a very good bottled mayonnaise in the supermarkets (in small jars, not bottles), with the brand name Benedicta. This recipe also makes an excellent light lunch.

4 large tomatoes	*quatres tomates*
200g (7oz) can of tuna	*une boîte de thon*
175ml (6fl oz) mayonnaise	*mayonnaise*
3 tablespoons chopped parsley	*persil*
salt, pepper	*sel, poivre*

Slice the tops off the tomatoes and scoop out the core, seeds and juice. Mix the tuna and mayonnaise in a bowl with a fork, adding the parsley, and season to taste. Stuff this mixture into the tomatoes, and chill until they are served. *(Serves 4)*

FOIE DE GENISSE

Fried calf's liver

*Foie de génisse (heifer's liver) and foie de veau (calf's liver)
both have a beautiful texture and are very quick to cook.
They are much less dry than lamb's liver. Rings of raw mild
onion (oignon doux) go well with this, as does chopped
spinach with triangles of fried bread. Fried potatoes and
braised celery or chicory (both with chopped walnuts) are
other ideas.*

400–500g (14oz–1lb) heifer's or calf's liver	*une livre de foie de génisse ou foie de veau*
thyme or wild thyme leaves	*thym ou serpolet*
1–2 tablespoons flour	*farine*
1 tablespoon olive oil	*huile d'olive*
2 tablespoons butter	*beurre*
salt, pepper	*sel, poivre*

Heat the oil and butter over high heat in a frying pan. Cut the
liver into thin slices, sprinkle them with thyme leaves, then
turn them in seasoned flour. Fry for 1–2 minutes on each
side, depending on thickness, and serve at once. *(Serves 4)*

CHAPTER NINE

CHILDREN AND BABIES

GETTING THERE

Many travellers in France think of the journey as a part of the holiday to be enjoyed, just like the rest, and that's fine. But it doesn't suit everybody, and in any case, the self-caterer has somewhere in particular to make for, a house or apartment that has to be paid for whether it's occupied or not. So the journey may need to be done as quickly as possible.

Now consider the arithmetic. The speed limit on French motorways is 130km/h (80mph). If you drive at the legal limit for ten hours without stopping you will cover 1300 kilometres (800 miles) – more than the distance from Calais to Cannes. In reality, with children, it can't be done. For one thing, you have to drive to the Channel and cross it. Then you find that the Europeans, out of step as usual, read the time from clocks set an hour in advance of the British model, so that the 8 a.m. ferry from Dover doesn't dock in Calais until 10.30, French time. By this time you've already been up for hours, and you're tired. Landing on French soil brings an undoubted energy boost, but what about the children?

Some children travel well, others don't. Some are happy to sit placidly all day and stare out of the window, while others start asking 'How much further?' a mile or so after leaving your own gate. You will know better than anyone what to expect from your own children.

To keep them occupied, it really is worth investing in a few games. If your children are old enough to play chess with each other you will probably have few problems anyway. But draughts, Scrabble and many other board games can be bought in a form which allows them to be played in a moving car. Simple games like I-spy, spotting particular landmarks and car number plates can work well enough, and many children seem to enjoy identifying the nationality of other cars from the identity discs stuck on the back. Following the map can also keep children occupied for a long time, and it has the added advantage that they have some idea of how long the rest of the journey is going to take.

French motorways provide far more opportunities for breaking your journey than British ones do. Service areas, with fuel and catering facilities, are about as common as they are in the UK (those with baby changing facilities are more common), but between each of these there are usually two or three smaller ones. These are invariably pleasantly landscaped, with little woods and grassy areas, picnic tables and playgrounds where children can let off steam and go to the loo. And if you establish a routine that after every stop there is a 'quiet time', you might even be rewarded by the sound of gentle snoring from the back seat afterwards.

Look for signs which say '*aire de. . .* [name]'. A picnic area is signed *pique-nique* and a children's playground is *jeux d'enfants*.

Some people travel by night, with the children fast asleep in the back. This brings with it the inevitable danger of driver fatigue and only you can decide if it's a possible answer for you and your family.

GENERAL NEEDS

Long before the drive, you will have asked and had answered several questions regarding your children's needs. If you need a cot (*un lit d'enfant*) you must enquire before you book. You're unlikely to find that one is provided as a matter of course, but the French can be extraordinarily obliging about things like this. The owner of the property may go to great lengths to find one for you, perhaps even borrowing one from a friend. It's often easier to negotiate this kind of thing, and be confident about it, if you have found the property from an advertisement rather than in a brochure, if only because you're then dealing directly with the owner rather than with an agent. If the property is British-owned, it's easier still.

LAUNDRY

Children create a lot of laundry, and arrangements for this, too, must be clear. Do you need a washing machine? Would a launderette do? There will certainly be one (*une laverie automatique*) in the local town. If you want a service wash, find a *blanchisserie* (laundry) or *blanchisserie-teinturerie* (laundry and dry cleaner), but this will be very expensive. (See LAUNDRY at the end of Chapter 10.) 'How much?' is '*Combien?*'. More expensive properties often include a maid service in the price, and even someone who takes care of the laundry. The only alternative is to take enough clothes with you not to need to wash any of them – but with two or three children this can amount to a small mountain! Whatever you decide, it's an important issue that has to be thought about before you leave.

NAPPIES *(couches or bébé-changes)*

Babies need nappies, and terry towelling nappies need washing. That much is sure. Disposable nappies, which are much more widely used now anyway, are easier, and are just as common in France. The best place to buy them is in a supermarket, where you will pay a little more than you would in an equivalent store in the UK. If you have to ask, they're called *bébé-changes* or *couches*. The major brands are international and easily found, and in addition there are several brands you probably won't have heard of. Naturally your British supermarket or chemist's own-label brand will not be available, and if you are dedicated to these you will have to take them with you. Sizes are standard. Talcum powder and cotton wool are easily found, but baby wipes are not, so if you use them, take a stock from home.

If your baby's bottle (*biberon*) or feeding cup goes missing, supermarkets again have a wide selection. Toddlers' feeding cups can seem very elaborate, but they work in just the same way, and your little one should adapt easily enough to the French style.

FOOD

Things have changed a lot in France in recent years. Not so very long ago it would have been possible to describe a typical French child's day and be fairly accurate. Nowadays there is no such thing, any more than there is in the UK. A few reminders of old France remain, such as the tendency for small children to sleep in the afternoon and stay up fairly late in the evening, often going out with their parents. But on the whole there is no discernible pattern. This is especially so in the case of food.

At one time the whole family sat down together and shared the same dish. The baby's food would be puréed. If this is what you do at home, there is nothing whatever to stop you doing so in France, too, and French food is just as suitable for children as British food.

All the same, convenience food is on the up and up. Prepared baby food, for example, is just as popular in France as it is in the UK. Dried food in packets, such as cereal and desserts, is usually quite cheap, whereas food in jars (tinned baby food is rare) is more expensive. The French demand rather more flavour from their food than the British do, and this applies to their babies, too. All the same, there is nothing outrageous about French baby food, and yours should find it quite acceptable. Babies have an inbuilt sense of self-preservation anyway and rarely go hungry for long.

It's usually older children who are a problem as regards food on holiday. If you take advice given elsewhere in this book you will eat well whether you stay at home or go to a restaurant, but you will eat what French people eat. The French demand a certain minimum standard of freshness, particularly as regards fruit and vegetables, but on the whole, the main difference between French food and our own is that they prefer stronger and more differentiated flavours. A simple piece of roasted meat may be accompanied by, say, courgettes. The meat will taste positively of meat and the courgettes of courgettes. For many francophiles, this kind of thing is the chief joy of visiting France. The same should apply to children, but all too frequently it does not.

Most of the average young Briton's favourite foods are available in France. Fish fingers (*bâtonnets de poisson*), burgers (*steak haché*) and frozen chips (*frites*) are all available in supermarkets. Whether your youngsters will like them, since they seem to have a stronger flavour than the British variety, is something else – although fish fingers are the same everywhere, as are cornflakes. Your offspring may well reject French sausages (especially the highly seasoned *merguez*) and French baked beans (*haricots blancs à la sauce tomate*), which are cooked in the familiar tomato sauce, but with different seasoning, and a different variety of bean is used to start with.

Many children are difficult to please at the best of times, and if yours are like this you will probably have problems with food in France. But it's a problem you should keep in perspective. What about you? Do you find the food acceptable? If the idea of chickeny chicken and fishy fish fingers doesn't appeal to you, maybe you shouldn't be going to France at all. If it does appeal, then it should appeal to your children too. If you are eating the French way, give them the same thing. If they reject it, they wait until the next meal. French food is different, but it isn't revolting – quite the reverse!

Having said all this, there are things that most children like, and seeking them out makes for a happy family and a happy holiday. French chocolate (*chocolat*) is expensive, and although there's nowhere near the variety that you see in an English newsagent's, it's all delicious. French crisps (*chips*) are excellent, available in huge bags, and very cheap, although there not many different flavours available. All the familiar canned soft drinks are very popular, and cordials, which have to be diluted, are common. *Sirop de citron* is lemon syrup, to which you add water. If *sucre* (sugar) doesn't appear prominently on the label, the drink will be tangy rather than sweet. Fruit juice (*jus de fruit*) is widely available in 1-litre (1¾-pint) packs.

Marmite is very difficult to find, and peanut butter is not so common, so take these with you if your children live on them. French jam is excellent. The nearest thing you will find to ordinary white bread is *pain de mie* (sandwich bread), which is normally displayed with the cakes. And it isn't all that much like our ordinary white bread. French cakes (*gâteaux*) are excellent, but not cheap. Biscuits (also *gâteaux* or *biscuits*) aren't cheap either, and are often more 'cakey' or crumbly, as the French seem less keen on crisp biscuits than the English.

HEALTH AND SAFETY

THE SUN *(le soleil)*

The South of France in the height of summer tends to be very hot and dry with long periods of clear skies. This is probably one of the reasons why you are going there. A lot has been written lately about the dangers of sunbathing, but, whatever your views on it, few French parents even think of subjecting their children to the sun, and you should follow local practice. In prolonged hot weather babies need considerably more fluid than normal, and they aren't well equipped to ask you for it. Older children can easily become dehydrated too, especially if they are running around enjoying themselves and don't think to ask for a drink.

It's important that they also have shade available, and are encouraged to use it regularly. This can be difficult. For any child going out in the sun, even for quite short periods, adequate sun protection is a must. Buy your anti-sun preparation at home, and buy more than you think you will need. Look for words like 'complete sun block' or anything which shows that the preparation is specially designed for children. Alternatively, go for the highest factor lotion you can find. Above all, don't think of it as a way of helping your child to get a suntan, but as a way of protecting your child from the sun. A suntan is undoubtedly attractive, but it is not a sign of good health, and is not something you should wish on your children.

If you assume that no anti-sun preparation will completely protect your child from the sun's rays, then you won't take any risks. If you run out, keep your children in the shade until you get some more. Supervised play, with lots of shade, is always safer than being in the sun, and will make for a less irritable child in the evening as well. A light T-shirt will give a little protection to the tender skin on the shoulders, and a wide-brimmed hat is a very good idea – if you can persuade your child to keep it on.

SNAKES *(les serpents)*

One thing we don't associate with France is snakes, but they can be quite common in tranquil, country areas and seeing one can be unnerving. Most of them are grass snakes *(couleuvres)*: harmless, though quite bad-tempered. They come out during the day, often basking quietly in the sun. Like all snakes, they don't like people, and will thrash away into the grass when you approach. Adders *(vipères)* are much more retiring, seek shade during the day and are active at night. They tend to avoid people too. If you disturb one, perhaps by turning up a stone, it may bite, thinking itself to be under attack. They are venomous, but the bite can be dealt with by a doctor with total success. Pack the wound with ice and go at once. This is one of many reasons (broken glass, sharp stones) why children should always wear shoes.

If your child becomes ill you can go along first to a chemist or, if you think it necessary, consult a doctor. For details of how to do this see in Chapter 11, under HEALTH.

BABYSITTERS *(le/la baby-sitter)*

On a happier note, you may want to abandon your children from time to time, either during the day or, more likely, in the evening. As with so many things, this is easier the closer you are to other people. In coastal and other established holiday resorts babysitting services may well have been set up. Ask for *quelqu'un pour garder les enfants* or *un baby-sitter*. Expect to pay 30F an hour or more. It's expensive, but you won't get a couple of teenage lovers. Organized play is also found, especially on the beach, and more often in special holiday villages than elsewhere.

If you are hiring a house in the depths of the French countryside, neither of these services will be laid on. The owner of the house, or even a neighbour, will probably know someone locally who would happily look after your children for an evening. This is as safe as it would be at home, and calls for exactly the same precautions.

If the idea doesn't appeal, you're better off forgetting it and taking your children with you, as the French themselves often do. It would be a very unusual restaurant that didn't make your children as welcome as it made you.

CHAPTER TEN

PRACTICAL HOUSEKEEPING

There are a few basic things that we take for granted at home but which, on holiday, need to be sorted out properly. You need to know what to do with your rubbish, for example, or how to work the water heater. And certain basic amenities, like the loo, must work properly. And if they don't, you need to know how to get them put right.

Housekeeping problems are likely to be more easily solved if you have an 'official' *gîte rural* in a village where your landlady or landlord lives, or which is on a farmer's property. If it is a *gîte rural* it has a constant flow of tenants who demand official standards. If the people who know how it all works are on the spot, they will be glad to keep an eye on things, for your sake and theirs.

In general, use your landlord (or the person in charge). Especially in country districts, she or he is interested in you and will be (usually) glad to give advice and help in such things as phoning for a doctor, recommending shops, laundries (but top-grade *gîtes ruraux* sometimes have washing machines) and restaurants, and suggesting excursions.

The usual expression for 'not working' or 'broken down' is *'ne marche pas'* (literally, 'doesn't go'). So *'l'aspirateur ne marche pas'* means 'the vacuum cleaner isn't working', and so on. Blocked is *bouché*, so if the sink is blocked, say *'l'évier est bouché'*. A good, sound, useful word in French is *problème*, problem. If you can't express what is wrong any other way, say *'Il y a un problème'* ('there's a problem'), then lead your landlord/lady gently to the source of the *problème*, and point.

A few useful words:

vacuum cleaner	*l'aspirateur*
sink	*l'évier*
wash-basin	*le lavabo*
lavatory	*la toilette*
blocked	*bouché*

RUBBISH *(les ordures)*

To begin with rubbish. There might be a dustbin (*une poubelle*), which someone else empties for you, or you might have to put the stuff in a plastic bag (*un sac en plastique*) and dump it in a swing-lid box not far away. In urban areas people bag up their rubbish and put it into large, wheeled dustbins that are emptied regularly. In rural areas there's often no bin, but bags are put out on the morning of collection day, which in the summer can be as often as every other day. Some communes are so small, however, that there's no rubbish collection at all, and householders make their own arrangements.

Whichever your situation, the question to ask is the same. Either '*Il y a une poubelle?*' ('Is there a dustbin?') or '*Qu'est-ce qu'on fait avec les ordures?*' ('What do we do with rubbish?'). If you don't understand, ask to be shown: '*Voulez-vous me montrer, s'il vous plaît?*'

Your property will almost certainly be provided with everything you need to keep it clean, but if you find you are short of anything, you can always ask – for example: either '*Avez-vous. . .*' (do you have. . .) or '*Je voudrais. . .* (I would like. . .) . . .*un balai, s'il vous plaît.*' (. . .a broom, please'). A bucket is *un seau*, and a cleaning cloth or duster is *un torchon*.

BOTTLED GAS *(gaz en cylindre)*

French country-dwellers are well accustomed to appliances that run on a cylinder of bottled gas *(un cylindre de gaz)*. If you are their first British tenants, they may not realize that such things can be bafflingly new to you. Don't worry unduly, because such things are meant to be fool-proof, in the sense that it ought to be difficult for you to set the place on fire. Make sure that you are shown how to work them.

There'll be a water-heater *(un chauffe-eau)* with a pilot light *(une veilleuse)*. Prudent French people would turn that off when they go out for the day, and perhaps at night. 'How do I light it?' – *'Comment est-ce que je l'allume?'* If one cylinder (the 13-kg sort that a strong person can shift) runs the cooker as well as the water heater, it won't last long. Wring your hands and cry *'Il n'y a plus de gaz!'* ('There's no more gas!') There might be a spare full cylinder next to the one that's connected. The French are used to changing these; but if you aren't, don't try. *'Veuillez le changer pour moi, s'il vous plaît?'* ('Will you change it for me, please?')

THE LAVATORY *(le WC)*

There ought to be no novelty, except in two cases – when you will almost certainly see a prominent notice near the seat in question. In both cases the notice is trying to tell you that NOTHING, ABSOLUTELY NOTHING (no, not even cigarette ends, tea-bags or tea-leaves, or a few spoonfuls of antiseptic) should be put in the lavatory, with the sole exception of your own bodily output and toilet paper.

One case is when there's a septic tank. Many French septic tanks are smaller than British ones and their users take great care to keep the beneficent bacteria that do the job in tip-top condition. Or else. . .

The other case is revealed when you have to press a button

to flush, and hear a whirring noise (as well as the usual one). A little motor is mincing up what you have put in, so that it can be sped along a narrow pipe – to, probably, a septic tank.

'The loo doesn't work!' – *'Le WC ne marche pas!'* ('It wasn't me!' – *'Ce n'était pas moi!'*)

ELECTRICITY *(l'électricité)*

Electricity often causes problems for British visitors to France. It can seem primitive, for one thing, as sockets anywhere else except in the kitchen and bathroom (yes, you do find sockets in the bathroom) have only two pins. But every French home has a preset limit to the power that can be consumed at any one time, and since the lower the limit the lower the standing charge, the French tend to opt for a lower limit and treat the electricity with respect. It amounts to making sure that the electricity being used at any one time is not more than the allowed limit. For example, your holiday home may have electric heaters (although this is unlikely), plus an electric cooker. The limit on the property will probably be 3kw, which means that if you had 2kw of electric heater going and you then switched on the electric oven, a further 2kw or so, the system would overload. No damage would be done, but everything would go off, lights and all, as the main switch trips if the system is overloaded. This can be very inconvenient, especially at night. It's not all that likely to happen, because these properties don't as a rule provide much in the way of electrical equipment, but it could. And if you have read elsewhere in this book that there won't be a kettle, and you decide to take your own, you should know that an electric kettle consumes around 2kw of power, which will probably be enough to trip the switch. . .

The electricity may well go off for other reasons too. Spectacular thunderstorms can occur, particularly in July and August, along the Mediterranean coast and also in some mountainous districts.

If the power suddenly goes off, have a look at the main switch, using the torch that you brought with you for just such an emergency. Instead of a main fuse there will be an overload cut-out switch, *un disjoncteur*. A sudden surge, caused by lightning, may have made it flip over. (It may be marked 0 and 1 instead of OFF and ON.) Just turn it on again. If turning it on produces no power, then the thunderstorm has also made a *disjoncteur* flip off somewhere further up the mains supply and you will just have to wait a while for the power to be restored to your district. (If, on the other hand, the *disjoncteur* refuses to let itself be switched on, something in the house circuit is performing the equivalent of blowing a fuse, and you are used to that sort of thing.) 'The electricity has gone off!' – *'Il n'y a plus d'électricité!'*

LAUNDRY *(la blanchisserie, la laverie automatique)*

If there's a washing machine provided (only in the top price brackets) or you're going to wash by hand, all you have to do is buy the powder *(la lessive)*. Finding powder in the supermarket is straightforward and many familiar lines are available. Otherwise, ask for *la blanchisserie*, and they'll do your washing for you. 'How much?' is *'C'est combien?'* To ask if they'll wash your things for you, say *'Veuillez laver ces affaires, s'il vous plaît?'* If you have to find a launderette, the expression is *une laverie automatique*.

CHAPTER ELEVEN

WHILE YOU'RE IN FRANCE

SURVIVAL SHOPPING

SHOPS

First, a note about shops where the items in this A–Z section are on sale. If medium-sized and big supermarkets stock them, your task is easy, because they are easily visible on the shelves. For some you have to go to:

THE CHEMIST *(la pharmacie)*

A *pharmacie* is not like Boots. It doesn't sell films or cassettes or toys or postcards or saucepans or Christmas decorations. It sells only pharmaceutical items, plus a few things like make-up and baby food in little pots, which you can get elsewhere. Some large *pharmacies* also sell homeopathic drugs, toiletries, perfumes and even veterinary products. Prices are high, so they are certainly not the place to buy suntan oil or baby's nappies on a regular basis.

The *pharmacie* is staffed by qualified *pharmaciens* who have to know about first aid and minor ailments; you can show your blister or insect bite or whatever to them and they will either sell you the right thing, doing their best to make you understand how to use it, or tell you that you ought to see a doctor *(un médecin)* and tell you where to find one.

Pharmacies have a big green cross, often illuminated, outside and the sign '*pharmacie*'. When closed, a notice on the door tells you where the 'duty chemist', *la pharmacie de garde*, is to be found.

Pharmacy is big business in France: the premises tend to be plush and the practitioners make a fair living. You will learn why if you get a headache. The price of aspirins will bring on another headache, so take a light medicine chest with you. (For payment, see HEALTH later in this chapter.)

HARDWARE SHOP *(la droguerie)*

La droguerie does not stock drugs or medicines. It deals in the non-metallic things you would find at a British ironmonger's.

IRONMONGER *(la quincaillerie)*

La quincaillerie sells metallic ironmongery – tools and so forth.

A–Z

- antiseptics for applying to skin and minor wounds: *la pharmacie* is the place. *Mercurochrome* is traditional for little boys' knees; bright red, it looks dramatic. But there are plenty of colourless ones. Ask for *une antiseptique* (if possible, show them what you want to use it on).
- aspirin (*comprimés d'aspirine*). You cannot get these, or any other medicament, at the supermarket or the corner shop. Go to *la pharmacie*.
- can opener (*ouvre-boîte*). From the supermarket or *quincaillerie*.
- condom (*le préservatif*). These can be found at *la pharmacie* and many other outlets, including slot machines, especially in places where tourists are thick on the ground.
- contact lens liquid (*la solution pour lentilles de contact*). From *la pharmacie*.
- corkscrew (*le tire-bouchon*). Look in the supermarket or *quincaillerie*.
- dental repairs. You will have to go to see *le dentiste*. It may cost a bomb, even with your E111 (it puts you in the same position as the French, who don't get much back on false teeth unless they're stainless steel crowns). French dentists are generally excellent; they tend to drive Porsches.

- do-it-yourself oddments. There are specialist shops, run on supermarket lines, for enthusiastic home handymen. Look for the sign *bricolage* (indeed, *Mr Bricolage* is one do-it-yourself chain). Minor items might be found at the ordinary supermarket if it's big enough. Otherwise, try *la quincaillerie*.
- elastoplast (*le pansement adhésif*). You can get this at the supermarket or *la pharmacie*.
- insecticide. An aerosol is *une bombe insecticide*; insect-repellent cream is *la crème anti-insecte*. Either can be found at the supermarket or *la droguerie*.
- motoring accessories. A selection will be on view at bigger supermarkets and at service stations.
- disposable nappies (*couches*). Familiar brands (Pampers, Peau-Douce) can be found at the supermarket or *la pharmacie*.
- pan scourers. Look in the supermarket for *éponges métalliques* or *éponges en nylon* or, more usually, various 'patent' names.
- make-up could be translated as *produits de beauté* or *maquillage*. It's cheapest and easily visible at the supermarket, mid-range at *la pharmacie*, and most expensive at a specialist shop, *la parfumerie*. Cleansing milk is *le lait de toilette*, moisturizer is *la crème hydratante* and foundation cream is *le fond de teint*.
- sanitary towels (*serviettes hygiéniques*). These are sold in the supermarket or *pharmacie*. Tampax has the same name. Little pads are *protège-slips*.
- Spectacles (*lunettes*). There are opticians (*opticiens*) clearly visible in every high street and they make a good living even though the customer gets little back on social security. A simple frame repair might be done for almost nothing by a kindly attendant, but lenses will almost certainly take a time and cost a bomb. Cheap sunglasses (*lunettes solaires*) are sold in the supermarket, expensive ones at the optician.
- underwear (*sous-vêtements*). Find cheap emergency replacements at bigger supermarkets, or expensive scraps of this and that where you see them in high street windows.
- watch battery (*la pile* – pronounced 'peel' – *pour montre-bracelet*). Any obvious watch/jewellery shop will sell them.

ANYTHING ELSE

The local *Syndicat d'Initiative* or *Office du Tourisme* very probably has someone who speaks English and knows about local shops as well as services (such as launderettes, bicycle hire, discos, acupuncturists, where to get a fishing licence. . .).

LOCAL SERVICES

BANKS *(le banque)*

Even the most experienced traveller in France can be defeated when it comes to using a bank! As a result, it's often a good idea, soon after your arrival, to establish which bank you are going to use, what it will do for you and when it will be open.

The main banks in France are Banque Nationale de Paris (BNP), Crédit Lyonnais, Société Générale and Crédit Agricole. In addition many towns will have a Caisse d'Epargne, essentially a savings bank (it has a squirrel as its emblem), which also offers exchange facilities. Even small towns have branches of most banks, and many villages have one too, often Crédit Agricole.

Core banking hours are from 9 a.m. until 4.30 p.m., Monday to Friday, with a two-hour lunch break from 12, but there are many variations on this theme, not all of them too predictable. Many branches of Crédit Agricole do not close for lunch; many banks do not open at all on Mondays; some are open on Saturday mornings. Some banks stop all foreign exchange transactions an hour or so before they actually close. You must be careful if your stay extends over a public holiday, as not only will banks close on that day, but may well close earlier than usual the day before. And if the holiday falls on a Tuesday, banks are closed all day on the Monday too!

DRAWING OUT MONEY

Most banks accept Eurocheques – '*Acceptez-vous les Eurochèques?*' ('Do you accept Eurocheques?') – although some branches of Crédit Agricole do not and individual branches of other banks may not be too happy with them. Some banks make a charge for this service, which is hardly fair, since your bank reimburses the French bank in full and you bear the charges.

Drawing out money on credit cards ought to be reasonably straightforward, but it often isn't. Visa is widely accepted, and Access/Mastercard is also accepted at places that take Carte Bleue, although less so than Visa. Bank staff sometimes shake their heads sadly as though they have never seen a card like yours before, and just because you used that particular card there last week doesn't mean to say that you can use it there this week! Cash dispensing machines displaying the relevant signs can also be used for drawing out money with these cards, but for some reason they often don't oblige. However you are trying to draw out money, you may be asked to show identification, to fill in a lengthy document of identity, both, or neither.

It used to be the case that you could do foreign exchange transactions only at certain desks. In most banks you can now go to any desk and show your credit card, travellers cheques or whatever. All the same, you may be directed to another desk, and if there is one that is clearly marked *change*, go there first.

TELEPHONE *(le téléphone)*

If you think you will want to use the telephone while you are in France, buying a phonecard *(une télécarte)* is a good idea now that fewer and fewer public phones take coins. You can buy cards at the post office, or from bars, newsagents, tobacconists, or anywhere that displays a *télécarte* sticker. If you're stuck, go into the nearest newsagent or tobacconist and ask: *'Avez-vous des télécartes, s'il vous plaît?'* ('Do you sell phonecards, please?'). If they don't, they'll direct you to someone who does.

Coin-operated phones can be found here and there. Airports and railway stations usually have them, and the smallest towns and villages seem to have retained them too. The minimum charge for making a call is 1F, and the coin boxes take ½F, 1F, 5F and 10F coins. There is usually a coin-operated phone inside the main post office and there may well also be a phone there that you can use and pay over the counter afterwards. This is useful if you're making a lengthy overseas call that would require lots of coins. Look in the booths: the phone you want will have no coin box or card slot. You should then go to the counter and say *'Je voudrais téléphoner, s'il vous plaît'*. Go back to the box, wait for a line, then continue as usual. After the call, pay at the counter.

CHARGES

Telephone calls are a little more expensive in France than in Britain. The charging periods are complicated, but the most expensive periods for calling within France fall between 8 a.m. to 12.30 p.m. and 1.30 to 6 p.m. during the week, and 8 a.m. to 12.30 p.m. on Saturdays. At all other times some kind of reduced tariff operates. There are only two charging periods for calling the UK. The reduced rate is from 9.30 p.m. through to 8 a.m. during the week, from 2 p.m. on Saturdays and all day Sunday. Calling England at the reduced rate from a public phone will cost in excess of 5F per minute.

USING A PHONECARD

Insert the card and a display will tell you how many units are available on the card. Then dial the number and proceed with your call. All French telephone numbers are of eight digits including the area code, and wherever you are in France, you dial only those eight digits. Paris is the only complication. If you are outside Paris calling a number inside Paris you must first dial 16, then wait for a second dialling tone (which may or may not appear instantly). You then dial 1 followed by the eight-digit number. If you are *in* Paris calling *out*, you dial 16 and wait for the tone, then the eight-digit number.

For phone calls to the United Kingdom and Republic of Ireland, see under CONTACT WITH HOME.

DIRECTORY ENQUIRIES

Directory enquiries in France are almost instant, and free – if you use the Minitel computer terminal provided at every post office (you'll need help the first time). But by phone it can be a very hit-and-miss affair, particularly if your French is not very good, and you have to pay. For directory enquiries within France dial 12, for the UK dial 19 33 12 44, and for the Republic of Ireland dial 19 33 12 353.

TRANSPORT

Most self-caterers on holiday in France have driven there, so the question of transport doesn't usually arise. All the same, there are times when members of a party want to go to different places and only one car is available. And when travellers staying in the country visit local towns and cities they usually leave the car securely parked and make their way around the town on foot, but it's good to know what transport is available if you want to use it.

In fact, public transport in France can be a hit-and-miss affair, especially in rural areas, although in cities it is generally excellent. Paris, for example, has the Métro, as well as a comprehensive network of buses. And to give another example, Toulouse, where the centre is small enough to walk almost anywhere, has an excellent bus service and a single line Métro is now under construction.

The problem is understanding how to use the system, as this varies widely from region to region. If you want to use public transport, either where you are staying or when you make a trip out, the best idea is to make straight for the tourist office (Syndicat d'Initiative). Quite small towns have these, and they are a mine of information. To find your local one, look for the tourist information sign, or use the yellow pages (*les pages jaunes de l'annuaire*), under *Offices de tourisme, syndicats d'initiative.* You will probably see leaflets there about the local transport services, but if you have to ask, the bus is *le bus*, the coach *le car*, the train *le train* and a taxi *un taxi*. (See also TRAINS in Chapter 3.)

FRENCH RAIL (SNCF)

SNCF offers a comprehensive service all over France, and with many cards and reductions available, a 50- or 60-km (30- or 40-mile) trip can work out cheaper for a group of people than it would going by car and taking the motorway. Any town that has a station will have several signs pointing to the station (*gare SNCF*), where you can ask for information (*des renseignements*).

COACH *(le car)*

There is a good coach network throughout France, but unlike Britain, this rarely works out cheaper than travelling by train, and is often more expensive. For information on this, you should go to your local coach station (*gare routière*).

VALIDATING YOUR TICKET

This is one point about French transport that often fools foreigners. Whether you are travelling by train or by bus, you're obliged to have your ticket stamped in a machine before you board the train or take your seat on the bus. You will see signs reminding you to *compostez* your ticket, which means to validate it in this way. If you fail to do so, you will be fined on the spot when the ticket inspector comes around. Don't rely on the inspectors being lenient because you're a foreigner and don't understand, you'll be treated in exactly the same way as a French person.

NEWSPAPERS *(les journaux)*

If you wish to read French newspapers while you are in the country, here's a brief guide. *Le Monde* is the most prestigious and intellectual, written in good, correct French – so probably the easiest to understand. Left-wing papers include *Libération* and *L'Humanité*, the former independent and idiomatic, the latter the paper of the Communist party. *Le Matin* is centre; all the other nationals (and most of the regionals) tend to the right. (For British newspapers, see later in this chapter, CONTACT WITH HOME.)

HEALTH

Public health, in the way of safe drinking water, inspection of beaches and legislation about the production, distribution and preparation of food, is by and large at least no worse than in Britain, and is in some ways a good deal better. Take the same precautions as at home, plus a few extra ones in the south in summer, as common sense dictates – for example, if mosquitoes are around (there are no malarial ones in France, but that's small comfort if all one wants to do is scratch).

It's a good idea to take a simple medicine chest and first aid kit with you, but sometimes your medicine chest might let you down. In this case, you have two options, either to go to a chemist (*pharmacie* – see SURVIVAL SHOPPING, earlier on) or to see a doctor. If it's a straightforward problem the chemist should be able to help you – they're well qualified for first aid. A chemist will not give you antibiotics without a doctor's prescription, so an infection of any kind warrants a call on the doctor. And naturally there are other problems that call for this too, especially if children are involved. You may find the following useful:

headache	*mal de tête*
stomach-ache	*mal d'estomac* or *mal au ventre*
backache	*mal au dos*
toothache	*mal aux dents*
vomiting	*vomissement*
diarrhoea	*diarrhée*
a cold	*un rhume*
sore throat	*mal de gorge.*

STOMACH UPSETS AND DIARRHOEA

Upset stomachs can be caused as much by too much sun as by the food, although children tend to double their fruit intake – and adults their wine intake – abroad. A day indoors, largely asleep, often works wonders.

In the case of diarrhoea, it's important to drink plenty of fluid to prevent dehydration. This is especially important for small children, and if you have an electrolyte powder (such as Dioralyte) with you, make use of it. If a bout of diarrhoea lasts for more than 24 hours, you should seek medical attention (see DOCTORS later in this chapter).

Kaolin tablets (*kaolin*) are an excellent corrective for diarrhoea caused by excess fruit and wine. As soon as the worst is past, eat some solid bready food. Lomotil (which you will need to bring with you, for it is on prescription) is the best medicine for stomach upsets caused by bugs in the water or bad hygiene.

If your stomach is sensitive, avoid anything with milk, cream, yoghurt or mayonnaise in it. And don't buy meat that has been displayed in the sun or in fly-infested areas.

KEEPING COOL

The evaporation of sweat from the skin is the body's way of cooling down. If you're in the south and it's hot, drink plenty of liquids (preferably water) to prevent dehydration. Children may protest that they're not thirsty, but ensure they drink at regular intervals. Take a siesta in the hottest part of the day. Wait until the late afternoon to sight-see or go to the beach.

SUN

Being in the sun can make you feel wonderful, but overdoing it can cause permanent damage to your skin. Not only can you get nastily burned, but a link has now been established between sudden, intense exposure to sun and skin cancer. You're most at risk if you have fair or freckled skin which burns before it tans, or if you have fair hair or light-coloured eyes. Protect yourself by:

- choosing a sunscreen that protects against both UVA and
- reapplying sunscreen at regular intervals (water and sweat will wash it away)
- using sunscreen on cloudy days; the sun is just as harmful

through cloud
- gradually building up the amount of time you spend in the sun; never stay in the sun until your skin goes red
- avoid sunbathing in the middle of the day when the sun is at its strongest
- covering up when you're walking round in the sun
- wearing a good pair of sunglasses to protect your eyes.

For bad burns, when the skin peels and the flesh turns scarlet, go to the *pharmacie* for advice. You may be recommended lanolin (*lanoline*) to smooth thickly on the affected area. Keep covered up and try to keep in the shade as well. Swim with a shirt on until the burns have healed.

SUNSTROKE

This is accompanied by headache and sickness. A day in bed in a darkened room, drinking juice usually cures it. Broken veins in the eyes, making them look yellow, are one temporary but unpleasant form, but polarized sunglasses help to prevent this.

STAYING SAFE

A few final tips to ensure that your holiday is happy and healthy.

- never let children in the water without at least one capable swimmer to keep an eye on them
- always check that the water is deep enough before diving
- stay away from animals that might bite or scratch – you risk catching rabies
- avoid riding motorbikes and bikes unless you have the right protective clothing
- make sure you know whom to contact in an emergency (see EMERGENCIES, Chapter 12).

DOCTORS

Doctors are thicker on the ground in France than in Britain. They will come to see you with alacrity (they get paid more for a 'home' visit). Any doctor listed in the yellow pages (*les pages jaunes*) of the telephone directory (*l'annuaire*) will be OK – ask a neighbour, your caretaker or your agent for a copy, or go to a bar or to the post office. They're very rarely available in public phone boxes.

The classification for doctors is '*médecins*', but there are several different kinds of doctor for you to choose from. *Médecins généralistes* are the equivalent of general practitioners. For a child, however, you might prefer to look under *médecins qualifiés: pédiatrie maladies des enfants* (qualified doctors: pediatrics, children's illnesses). Gynaecologists are listed as *médecins qualifiés: gynécologie médicale* and obstetricians as *médecins qualifiés: gynécologie-obstetrique*.

Acupuncturists (*acupuncture*) and homeopaths (*homéopathie*) are also listed, and you may consult these if you wish. It should be emphasized that these are not specialists in the usual British sense. They are usually doctors who have undertaken further study in a specialist area, such as pediatrics, and whose practice is normally confined to treating cases in that speciality. You can consult them without being referred by another doctor.

The procedure for visiting a dentist is exactly the same. Look up *dentistes* in the *annuaire*.

Don't forget that French telephone directories list people according to where they live, so after you have found the doctors' listing, you then look under the nearest town or village to where you are staying.

VISITING THE SURGERY

If you go along to the surgery you may be able to sit and wait. Say '*Je voudrais voir le docteur, s'il vous plaît*' ('I'd like to see the doctor, please'). If you can't be seen then and there, you will have to make an appointment (*un rendez-vous*). Describing your symptoms in French can be tricky, but don't worry unduly. Most doctors understand English, especially medical English, if it's spoken clearly – and if they can do a lot when you're unconsious, they can do that much more if you can say 'ouch!'.

PAYMENT

For goodness' sake make sure that you are covered by insurance – both as a citizen of the EC with your form E111 and, on the belt-and-braces principle, with a modest private insurance (see FREE HEALTH CARE WITHIN THE EC – FORM E111 in Chapter 4). With either or both you will have to stump up first, paying doctor, chemist and hospital (the latter within reason – a hospital may be willing to wait a while for its bill to be settled) and getting your money back later. So make sure that you have some emergency cash or quick access to it. Private insurance can get you back to Britain in a hurry if that's what is needed.

A simple consultation will cost between 80F and 120F. Keep the receipt the doctor gives you, and ask for a receipt in the chemist too, if one is not offered. You will need these when you make your claim back at home. A bill is *une facture*, a receipt is *une quittance*, and a prescription is *une ordonnance*.

DRIVING

If you enjoy driving, but can't remember what a clear road was like, then France is the country for you. You can drive for mile after mile in rural France and hardly see another car.

It's important that you try to avoid travelling during the weekends of July and August, though, especially the outside weekends of August, because it's then that huge numbers of French travel to and from their own annual holiday. Motorways in the south are the worst affected, especially those leading to the borders of Spain and Italy, but the knock-on effects of serious jams can block other roads too, and the road system as a whole gets very congested. So do your travelling in the week if at all possible.

Empty roads tempt people to drive at speed, and some French drivers give in to the temptation. They can overtake at times which seem to us unsafe, and will frequently approach you very fast from behind on the overtaking lane of motorways, often with flashing of lights. You may not like this, but it's quite normal to them, and they'd probably be surprised to know that it made you angry. You can wait for a long, long time before anyone slows down or stops to let you out of a difficult turning, and if you try to do that kind of favour for someone else, the driver may appear not to understand what you are doing. Even if he does, he will probably not give you the gesture of thanks you are used to.

PEDESTRIAN CROSSINGS

Being a pedestrian can be a challenge, especially when it comes to crossing the road. If you use a pedestrian crossing, traffic is supposed to give way to you, but only once you are on the crossing. In practice they give way only if you are directly in their path, so if you take two or three tentative steps onto the crossing and then wait, drivers will ignore you. Wait on the kerb for traffic to stop and you will wait all day. Not surprising, then, that French pedestrians don't bother with the crossings all that much, and in any case, drivers' behaviour seems to differ very little whether there's a pedestrian crossing or not.

It's not at all uncommon, in towns, to see cars stopping to let pedestrians cross in front of them even where there is no crossing. If you're not happy with this cut and thrust system, be sure to wait until the road is quite clear before you attempt to cross, remembering always that the traffic approaches you first from the left. Alternatively, you can use a pedestrian crossing with lights. But if the crossing is at a road junction, you should be careful here too. You may have a green light indicating you can go, but quite often traffic turning into the junction, in other words, towards you, may also go, but have a flashing light indicating that they must give way to pedestrians. They invariably do give way, but they can approach you very quickly, which can be pretty unnerving.

Apart from these peculiarities, the French drive perfectly well, and the best advice is to keep calm and not let their unfamiliar ways annoy you.

SPEED LIMITS

Speed limits for cars (*voitures*) are 90km/h (56mph) on single carriageways, 110km/h (68mph) on dual carriageways and 130km/h (80mph) on motorways. These limits are reduced in wet weather to 80km/h (50mph), 100km/h (62mph) and 110km/h (68mph). The speed limit in built-up areas, unless otherwise indicated, is 50km/h (31mph) and on urban stretches of motorway 110km/h (68mph). Motorists towing caravans or trailers of any sort are subject to reduced speed limits according to the weight of the trailer, and should check these before driving on French roads.

Speed checks are increasingly carried out by the French police, and if caught speeding you will be fined on the spot. Severe offences are punishable by confiscation of the driving licence.

DRINKING AND DRIVING

If you drive you shouldn't drink. If you insist on doing so, be warned that the limits are stringent, and the random, roadside Alcotest, in which all cars travelling in both directions are stopped, are quite common. The legal limits in France are 0.8g per thousand in blood and 0.4mg per litre in exhaled air. Drivers who are over the limit are liable to heavy, on-the-spot fines (up to 30,000F) or a custodial sentence. It can also lead to confiscation of your licence and immobilization of the car on the spot. Handing over your keys at midnight on an unlit country road several kilometres from home is probably not the best way to round off an enjoyable evening.

PARKING

Parking (*parking*) is rarely much of a problem. The regulations are complex, but parking is simple in practice, at least outside the larger towns and cities. Even there, multi-storey and underground car parks are clearly signposted and are often clean and safe, although things can be very different in parts of Paris, Marseilles and some of the heavy tourist centres. Parking meters (*horodateurs*) are also used, and disc parking is in operation in some places, but this can be complicated and a multi-storey is simpler.

In smaller towns and villages you can usually pull up wherever you want to, subject to local practice and your own common sense. Having said that, failure to observe the local parking restrictions can result in heavy fines, or having your vehicle towed away. Local police are unlikely to be lenient towards vehicles with a GB plate. Some streets have parking on alternate sides of the road according to what day it is. In this case you should follow the herd.

The main square is often used for parking in many small towns, but not on market days. Do not park anywhere that you see a sign saying '*stationnement interdit*' with a 'P' in a circle and a line through it, or where the kerbs are marked with yellow paint, or where you see a red circle and red diagonal line on a blue background. Parking in these smaller towns is almost always free.

PETROL *(l'essence)*

You should have no problems finding petrol, as filling stations are common on main roads, motorways, in towns and on the outskirts. You will see many signs directing you to filling stations, even on country roads, but if you are doing a lot of travelling in rural areas it makes sense not to let the tank get too low, as garages in these regions have rather haphazard opening hours. Petrol bought at filling stations in the heart of the country and on the motorway will be the most expensive.

Price varies widely, and the cheapest petrol is often found at out of town supermarkets and hypermarkets. Two grades of petrol are available: *essence*, which is roughly equivalent to 2-star, and *super*, which is roughly equivalent to 4-star. Lead-free petrol, which had a slow start in France, is now widely but not universally available, and at the time of writing is only fractionally cheaper than leaded petrol. Look for *sans plomb* and green pumps. Diesel *(diesel)* is always available. It costs about two-thirds the price of petrol, and many French people drive diesel cars.

More filling stations have attendants than in the UK. To ask for the tank to be filled, say *'le plein, s'il vous plaît'*. A peculiarity of many French self-serve filling stations is that you have to wait until the person who used the pump immediately before you has paid before the cashier will reset the pump to zero. This can result in a rather frustrating wait by the side of your car in a large garage that is very busy.

If you want to pay for your petrol by credit card, Visa and Mastercard (Access) are widely accepted. Don't automatically assume acceptance of cards, though, especially in small country garages, but look for the signs. Many garages accept Eurocheques, but you should certainly not rely on this. In fact, you are best advised to have enough cash on you to pay for your petrol that way if all else fails. Many garages that accept cards use the automatic 'wipe-through' system, which rejects foreign cards with monotonous regularity.

BREAKING DOWN

Breaking down on holiday is an utter nuisance and can turn into a nightmare. Motorways and many other major roads are well served for emergency telephones, but you may well be doing much of your driving on deserted country roads, which are not. Being reduced to flagging down other motorists for a lift to the nearest telephone is no fun at all on holiday. Have your car fully serviced a couple of weeks before you leave. If you are any good at these things, identify those components whose malfunction you could diagnose yourself and which you could replace at the roadside if necessary, and carry a spare set with you.

Parts for non-French cars are often very expensive, so a set of basic parts is probably a good idea even if you are no mechanic yourself. The AA and RAC will advise on this.

If you do break down, emergency telephones are connected to the police, who will contact a garage for you. You can of course choose a garage yourself, but since you are unlikely to know any, it's much better to take all possible steps to avoid breaking down in the first place.

I have broken down	*Je suis en panne*
I've got a puncture	*J'ai un pneu crevé*
There's something wrong with the brakes/clutch/accelerator	*J'ai un problème avec les freins/l'embrayage/l'accélerateur*
How long will it take?	*Cela prendra combien de temps?*

SECURITY

Rural France can feel like a blissful haven of safety for the harrassed British town dweller, and the chances of your car being stolen or broken into in such an area are remote. All the same, the French are themselves very security-minded; most French people would never dream of leaving their car unlocked in town, and you should follow their example. Objects left visible, particularly in a foreign car, will attract attention, so wherever possible you should lock everything in the boot if you cannot take it out of the car.

A car left in a busy street is less likely to attract attention than one in a car park, but you will have to judge this for yourself according to the 'feel' of the area. As with so many topics in this book, the rule for big centres and heavy areas of heavy tourist concentration is different from the rule in the country.

HIRING A CAR

You may decide not to drive your own car but to hire one instead. This certainly has some advantages, not least the fact that you sit on same side of the car as everyone else.

Major car hire companies are international, and desks are found at airports and the main railway stations. Car hire is a good 20% more expensive than in the UK, but you can pick up quite remarkable bargains by shopping around at home. Many British travel companies work in conjunction with French car hire firms, and can offer very good deals. Look in the small ads of your local paper for this, but don't neglect your travel agent either, as most of the larger travel companies also offer a scheme of their own. Telephone one of the bigger companies at the airport nearest to your destination to compare prices. French for car hire is *location de voitures*.

In theory you should be able to turn up at the airport and book your car there and then. Your annual holiday will be more carefully planned than this, though, and booking is essential. Paying for the car before you leave can also help with your budgeting, as there should be no more unexpected costs. If you have a special requirement, and your holiday can't proceed without it, such as a baby seat (*un siège-bébé*) you should naturally specify this on booking. (See also Chapter 3, HIRING A CAR.)

CONTACT WITH HOME

POST *(la poste)*

The natural way most holidaymakers make contact with home is by sending postcards. But many people like to phone, and those who simply can't bring themselves to forget about work might even want to send a fax.

Buying postcards *(cartes postales)* is easy. You can get the stamps *(timbres)* for them at the post office or from most tobacconists *(tabacs)*. The main post office is often a fairly imposing building with a large yellow sign on it saying *La Poste*, but if you want to ask where it is, simply say *'Où est la poste, s'il vous plaît?'* It costs the same to send a postcard or a lightweight letter to England as it does within France, currently 2F30. You can buy stamps in books of ten *(un carnet)*. As in Britain, they don't work out any cheaper, but are easier to ask for.

Carnets are usually only available from the post office, and this can involve a lengthy wait – the tobacconist is quicker. If you do go to a post office, be sure that you are waiting in the correct queue. Look for signs saying *timbres, toutes opérations* (all services) or *autres opérations* (other services) and you should be all right. Post your cards early on if you want to be sure they arrive home before you do.

TELEPHONE AND FAX *(le téléphone et le fax)*

There are all sorts of reasons why you might want to ring home. For general advice on how to use the public telephones in France see LOCAL SERVICES earlier in this chapter. To make a call home you first dial 19, which gives you access to the international network. Wait until you hear a second dialling tone (though it may appear instantly) and then dial the country code – 44 for the UK or 353 for the Republic of Ireland. Now dial the number you are calling, including the domestic code but omitting the initial 0. For example, to call Leeds (0532) 123456 dial 19 44 532 123456. To make a reverse charge call, dial 14 for the operator and say '*Je voudrais téléphoner en PCV*'.

For those who want to send a fax, there will be facilities, in larger towns and cities, in business hotels. In smaller towns, shops that sell office furniture and equipment (often called *bureautiques*) usually offer photocopying and fax facilities. The cost of this varies very widely, but it does tend to be very expensive. The word 'fax' is widely used and understood in France, but a fax machine is *un télécopieur*.

TELEGRAM *(le télégramme)*

Telegrams are little used now, but if you do need to send one it should be possible to do so from a public phone by dialling 36 55. In practice, though, it would work out much better to do it face to face at the post office. Start off by saying '*Je voudrais envoyer un télégramme, s'il vous plaît*' ('I want to send a telegram, please').

ENGLISH NEWSPAPERS AND RADIO

Getting away from it all is one thing, but losing touch is another, and many like to be able to keep up with the news at home. In any town where there are tourists there is usually at least one newsagent that sells English newspapers – look for *maison de la presse*. The papers generally arrive during the afternoon of the day of publication, or the next morning, and cost about three times as much as they do at home.

You can hear the national radio stations on FM throughout most of northern France, and on AM until quite far south, and there is also the BBC World Service. This you can receive anywhere in France provided you know the best wavelengths to tune in to. The BBC publishes a free leaflet giving information that you can get from BBC External Services, Bush House, Strand, London WC2, before you go.

CHAPTER TWELVE

EMERGENCIES

EMERGENCY TELEPHONE

If there's an accident and you need to call for an ambulance, dial 15 – but check this number when you arrive, as it sometimes varies according to which part of France you are in. The ambulance service is called SAMU. Say '*J'ai besoin d'une ambulance, s'il vous plaît*' ('I need an ambulance please').

Many French people ring the Fire Brigade (*les pompiers*) first, especially if the problem stems from an accident. The firemen will bring a doctor with them if necessary. And of course you call the Fire Brigade if there is a fire. Dial 18.

For the police, dial 17.

USEFUL PHRASES

You always hope that you won't need to call any of these numbers. But if you do, and your French is not up to explaining what you need, here are some phrases that might be useful. It's worth becoming familiar with them before you need them, since you'd be very unlikely to start leafing through this book to find out how to ask for a doctor/ambulance/police/fire brigade when you've just driven into a tree/had your bag snatched/cut your finger.

Where is the nearest telephone?	*Où se trouve le téléphone le plus proche?*
There's been an accident	*Il y a eu un accident*
People are hurt	*Il y a des blessés*
Call a doctor/ambulance	*Appelez un médicin/une ambulance*

child	*enfant*
sick	*malade*
fire	*incendie*
doctor	*docteur*
car	*voiture*

If your French is poor, find a French person or someone who speaks French well to aid you. However urgent your situation is, this may well get help to you more quickly than if you tried to contact the emergency services direct. So throw yourself on the mercy of a French neighbour – you're unlikely to be turned away.

If you have to call the emergency service yourself, try to keep as calm as you can, though this is easy to say out of the situation. Say where you are (*'je suis à. . .'*) and what the problem is, even if only single words will come.

HOSPITALS, DOCTORS AND DENTISTS

Perhaps you have cut your finger badly, or have a problem that is best treated in the casualty department (*les urgences*) of a hospital (*un hôpital* or *centre médical*). Find out where the hospital is when you first arrive at your holiday home (the road signs indicating hospitals are marked with a red cross).

Procedures vary from hospital to hospital and from town to town. If your French is good enough, you can telephone first, but if you simply present yourself and display your symptoms, the duty staff will tell you what to do.

AT NIGHT

It's often the case that emergencies, large or small, occur at night, and there are usually particular doctors, dentists and nurses on call during the night in particular localities. They'll be listed in your local paper (*le journal régional*), on the page which features news of your nearest small town. There, above

213

the pictures of football teams, visits and community outings, there should be a separate box containing useful local information, including the names and numbers of the people you are likely to need.

LOSS AND THEFT

If your car is stolen, go to the police station nearest to where you last left it and say '*On a volé ma voiture.*' ('Someone has stolen my car.')

Similarly, if you lose something valuable, the police station is the place to go. '*J'ai perdu. . .*' means 'I have lost. . .', and whether it's your *montre* (watch), your *collier d'or* (gold necklace) or your *parapluie* (umbrella), you may be told to go away and come back again tomorrow, and the next day, and the next; or you may be asked to go through a procedure rather like making a statement, with much filling in of forms and signing of names. If your property is returned to you after all that, think of it as a lucky bonus.

INSURANCE

As a general rule, make sure that you take your insurance policy with you and any emergency telephone numbers they supply you with. If you are going to make any sort of claim, keep all receipts and documentation carefully and, in the case of theft or loss, make sure that you have made a report to the police or your claim may be void. (See also Chapter 4, GETTING READY.)

CREDIT CARDS

The minute you discover that your credit card is missing, phone the 24-hour 'lost and stolen' number. Report it at home, not in France (apart from American Express – see below).

The lost and stolen numbers for the UK are:

VISA   19 44 604 230230
ACCESS   19 44 702 362988
AMERICAN EXPRESS   19 44 273 696933 (or look in
                              the phone book and contact
                              any local American Express
                              office)

If you have no cash, dial the operator and ask for a reverse charge call (*téléphoner en PCV*). The credit card company will accept the call.

TRAVELLERS CHEQUES

When you get travellers cheques, you get a record sheet and instructions about what to do in case of loss or theft – it really is wise to hang on to these and keep them safe. You must keep a record of the cheque numbers and of the ones you've used, so that you know exactly which ones are lost. If not, a lost cheque is like a lost banknote – gone and irreplaceable.

You will have been given a form with instructions about what to do in case of loss. For American Express, contact the nearest office, and the cheques will be replaced (after much form-filling). If your travellers cheques are from a bank or building society and you don't have the instructions about what to do, go to a French bank or a branch of any UK bank, and they may be able to put you on the right track. The tourist office in a large centre may also have some useful addresses. You can also use the international directory enquiries to find out the number of your bank at home and phone direct.

CONSULAR SERVICES

If you need special help when you are abroad in an emergency you should contact the British Consul. There are many things that the British Consulate can do. They can issue emergency passports, advise on the transfer of funds, provide lists of local doctors, lawyers and interpreters, give advice and contact relatives in the event of the death of one of your party and give advice if you are arrested while in France.

However, the consul can not ensure preferential treatment for you if you are in prison or hospital, or give legal advice. The consul will not pay hotel and medical bills but will, as a last resort, give a loan for your return to the UK. It will be able to supply you with a new passport or documentation to get you back home.

The address of the British Consul in France is given in Chapter 3, USEFUL ADDRESSES, although there may be one nearer to where you are staying. The consulate in Paris will be able to give you this information.

CHAPTER THIRTEEN

BUYING THINGS TO TAKE HOME

France is a large country, and almost everywhere something or other is produced which seems particularly characteristic of the region, and buying it will bring back happy memories of your trip. Whether it's perfume from Grasse, mustard from Dijon, dried herbs or patterned fabrics from Provence or nougat from Montélimar, you won't be disappointed if you choose carefully. Things which you buy to take home normally fall into two categories: those items that are available at home but which are cheaper in France, and those things that are particularly French – to remind you of your holiday in the dark, wintry days to come.

FOOD

What most people would like to take home from France is a representative selection of French food. Unfortunately the law forbids the importation of most fresh food, so you have to stick mostly to tins and jars. Having said that, many people take home garlic, a string of which lasts for weeks in a cool spot, and to leave France without a little cheese seems almost perverse. You will have decided which cheeses you like best, and they travel well enough, though make sure they don't get too hot, especially the soft cheeses, otherwise you will know about it!

As for tinned food, *cassoulet*, that heavy, filling south-western stew, makes a superbly warming and evocative supper on a cold English evening, and some tinned varieties are not bad. Rather more refined, but from the same region, are the preserved meats. *Confit de canard* is preserved duck and *confit d'oie* is goose. Pork is cheaper and just as good. Meat which is cooked and preserved this way really is delicious, and if you try it while you are in France you're bound to want to take some home with you. *Foie gras* too, not to mention the more robust, peasant-type *pâtés*.

A less obvious choice is tinned vegetables. These are quite cheap, and are really far superior in flavour to almost anything you can get at home. *Petits pois* (peas) are available in various grades – *fin*, *extra-fin*, etc. (fine, extra-fine) – and the very best products are sold in jars. These tend to be a bit more expensive.

It would be a pity to spend a holiday within striking distance of Marseilles and not take home a can or two of excellent *bouillabaisse*, or some *choucroute* from the regions close to the German border. And if your taste is more towards sweet things, the French do a wonderful line in chocolate and truffles. As with many things, if you go to one of the special *chocolatiers* that you are bound to see in your local town, you will come away with a beautifully wrapped selection of delicious chocolates, but they will be quite expensive. Wonderful for a treat or a present, but for filling the boot you would be better to scour the supermarket shelves once more.

DRINK

Most things are in fact rather more expensive in France than they are at home, and the obvious choice of moneysaving items is drink. Since wine is so easy to buy at home now, and the choice is so wide, many people prefer to look out for the more interesting liqueurs and spirits, or even some of that lovely, fizzy cider from Normandy.

UK CUSTOMS ALLOWANCES

The first thing to grasp is that your allowance is larger if bought outside a duty-free shop, because it has already paid tax in the country of origin. Duty-frees are mainly for travellers by air and ship. Champagne will be classed as part of your spirits allowance.

If you are travelling by car, and want to carry your entire allowance in wine, two people are allowed 16 litres (28 pints) – that is, 21 bottles of 75ml size, if bought in French shops or from a producer. But remember, if you do this, you can't then take any other duty-free alcohol.

ALLOWANCES FROM DUTY-FREE SHOPS

- 1 litre spirits, liqueurs, etc. over 22%
  or
  2 litres not over 22% (sparkling wine)
  plus
  2 litres still wine

  OR

- 4 litres still wine only

ALLOWANCES FROM FRENCH SHOPS

- 1.5 litres spirits, liqueurs, etc. over 22%
  or
  3 litres not over 22%
  plus
  5 litres still wine

  OR

- 8 litres still wine only

CRAFTS

If your holiday is in the Pyrenees or close by, Pyrenean wool is a good buy. You can take it home ready to knit into something yourself, or already made up into jumpers, scarves, gloves and caps. A particularly good idea for cold winter evenings can only be described as a pair of mittens for the feet. It's like a single, huge woolly slipper that you slip both feet into. They really are beautifully warm, but you have to be careful if you get up suddenly to go to the door or answer the phone, as it's easy to forget that your feet are effectively tied together!

The Basque region, especially around St Jean de Luz, produces the most beautiful embroidered tablecloths and napkins. They are not exactly cheap, but considering the work that goes into them, they're not too expensive either. They don't seem to turn up in English shops, and visitors are guaranteed to admire them on your table.

A traditional way of covering the table in France used to be oilcloth. Nowadays it's vinyl, and it's manufactured and sold throughout France in bright, cheerful colours. It's informal and practical – you just wipe it clean – and is ideal for everyday use in the kitchen. You'll see it displayed on huge rolls in the market, and in department and hardware stores. If you can't find it, ask for *la toile cirée*.

BAGS AND BOOKS

Keep a lookout for things that are out of the ordinary. If you can use them every day at home, reminding yourself of your French trip as you do so, all the better. For example, your children might have noticed that French schoolchildren carry their books to school in brightly coloured satchels and briefcases (you see these for sale almost everywhere in the second half of the summer break). They aren't expensive and would be fun to take home – and would give your children a little extra kudos with their peers at school.

A good idea which people often forget, for some reason, is books. French books can seem expensive, especially the kind of mass-market ones that are often quite cheap in England.

But there are few better ways of improving your French than reading the language, and few more pleasant ways of recalling a holiday than by browsing through a beautifully illustrated book about the region you stayed in. Books are *livres*, and a bookshop is *une librairie*.

KITCHEN THINGS AND POTTERY

French cookware always seems cheap to British travellers, especially enamelled cast iron casseroles and saucepans which can cost two-thirds of the UK price, and sometimes even less.

Pottery (*céramique*) is always popular, and this is again something that you actually use when you get home. Certain regions specialize in the production of pottery. In Brittany, for example, the style is rustic and fairly heavy, but charming and practical at the same time. If you like the idea, and decide to take home more than just a couple of pieces, it's a good idea to go to the factory (*l'usine*) and buy it from there.

Almost every region of France has a range of pottery of its own, but none if more famous than the porcelain of Limoges. It is wonderfully delicate, and many believe it to be the finest in the world. If it appeals to you, a carefully chosen set would be a most elegant and lasting reminder of your trip to France.

Index